MARGI

Now you see me...

MARGI

Now you see me...

Memoirs of a
working class Diva

TrinityMirror Media

The time has come for me to tell it like it was.
And is...

I'm not a budding Shakespeare
or even a Jackie Collins.
But I will endeavour to tell the tale of the
Kirkby girl with a strong imagination.

Margi Clarke,
2010

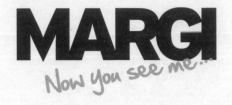

MARGI
Now you see me...

TrinityMirror Media

Acknowledgements

MARGI: NOW YOU SEE ME...
Copyright Margi Clarke
Book Editor: Peter Grant
Produced by Trinity Mirror Media
Business Development Director: Mark Dickinson
Executive Editor: Ken Rogers
Senior Editor: Steve Hanrahan
Editor: Paul Dove
Art Editor: Rick Cooke
Production/proofing: James Cleary, Mike McGuinness
Assistant Book Editor: Vicky Andrews
Designer: Zoe Bevan
Additional research: Cathy Roberts and Brian Johnston
Sales and Marketing Manager: Elizabeth Morgan
Sales and Marketing Assistant: Karen Cadman
Marketing Executive: Claire Brown

Front cover image: Mirrorpix
Trinity Mirror Media,
PO Box 48, Old Hall Street, Liverpool L69 3EB.
ISBN: 9 781906 802523
Photographs: Margi Clarke personal collection.
Liverpool Daily Post and ECHO, Mirrorpix, Carlton TV, Thames.
Printed by: CPI Mackays, Chatham ME5 8TD

Contents

The Chameleon

Introduction by Peter Grant

I have known her for 30 years and, in that long time, our paths have always crossed.

"How are yer doing, lad?" she always asks.

"How are you, girl?" I say.

We are old friends.

Margi seems to be old friends with everyone she meets.

This chameleon – Margi with a hard not soft 'G' Clarke – has refused to be labelled by any one thing. Any one genre. Film actress, singer, soap star, panto queen, broadcaster, poet, stand-up, philosopher, health guru – even a journalist.

And a Gemini.

Journalist – yes – who else could land world exclusive chats with Hollywood megastars Michael Douglas and Jack Nicholson?

Maybe 'land' should be replaced by 'blag' – that's more our Margi.

From her earliest incarnation as rebel-with-a-cause Margox, to the world-famous, mould-breaking film Letter to Brezhnev, her career has been up and down more times than the British economy.

But she has a never-say-die attitude.

A home spun philosophy of: "Look, give it a go and try and if you fail, just dust yourself off and start again." She may have been down-hearted and through some emotional turmoil – but she refuses to let it show.

Margi has never really been off our screens, small and big ones (I can hear her infectious laugh now, as she throws her pink head back at the very thought). "Small and big ones, what are yer like, kid?!" From TV soaps like Brookside, Family Affairs and – the big one – Coronation Street, Margi has shown her versatility.

She cut her showbiz teeth (and lost a load, but more of that later) as a stunning presenter with Granada TV with the late, great, inspirational Anthony H Wilson, and then went on to establish a singing career. Margox was a revelation as a punk presenter and she opened the door for other styles of music shows, as seen on The Tube and The Word.

She hosted The Good Sex Guide for Carlton TV, she won awards and she rightly beat all competitors for Best TV Presenter. What an achievement in such a competitive field.

There were TV dramas such as BBC's Soul Survivors with Ian McShane and the classic series Making Out, that again saw a way of making good telly with real characters we can all relate to. And we all know someone like Queenie, one of Margi's other alter egos.

As for the films, well, Letter to Brezhnev changed the British film industry forever. What other film could have the star and her brother at the helm, and the mam doing the catering? Family means everything to Margi Clarke.

After that she worked on a trilogy of art films and then, in her own inimitable way, openly and honestly declared she "couldn't even get arrested." Blonde Fist, about a feisty female boxer and written by brother Frank, is still a cult film. Years later there was School For Seduction with a top-notch cast including Kelly Brook. We saw a softer Scouse Margi – she turned the volume down, so to speak.

Then there's reality, non-drama show Margi being Margi.

The Weakest Link, The Farm, Celebrity Total Wipeout and Cash in the Attic. Producers know that the minute she appears on screen she stamps her own personality. Full stop.

She met a Beatle, had a hit record and she also asked Jack Nicholson if he wanted some 'medical attention'. But that's for Margi to tell you in her own wonderful way with her own words.

I recall interviewing her back in the 1990s when she was concerned about her hometown's future. She came up with a vision of Liverpool as a big ship sailing into unchartered new waters.

In detail she described the horizon – which way it was going and the impending storms. On board were the movers and shakers. It was a positive, uplifting piece and it came true. The city became European Capital of Culture and Margi was there on the celebration night in 2008 ...sparkling, laughing and not once saying: "I told you so."

Her life has seen much tragedy and, yet, she has an inner strength that pulled her through and still pulls her through now.

There are scars as well – bound to be. It's a tug of love with Margi not war.

Anyone who meets her will know that she responds with a genuine warmth and affection – that is so real. She only has to go walkabout in any city centre in the country and people will come up and say: "Hi Margi." And she will have a right old gab. "Alright girl," and "See yer, lad." She might cadge a ciggie...but she will then light up with optimism.

And this is where I came in...

Margi Clarke is an easy person to interview because the anecdotes and the tales come flooding out, from the hilarious to the sensitive, the sublime to the utterly ridiculous.

This book is called Now You See Me. Many readers will 'see' and 'hear' Margi for the first time as she really is. It's Margi by Margi.

Margaret Mary Bernadette Clarke is a survivor and creative chameleon.

Now you see her – well, you ain't seen or heard nothing yet.

Peter Grant, 2010

NOW YOU SEE ME

How to become invisible
How to become see through
How to become brand new
Change your name

A poem by
Margaret Mary Bernadette Clarke

I Wanna Be Loved By You

Foreword by Margi Clarke

'I wanna be loved by you
Just you and nobody else but you
I wanna be loved by you, alone...'

I was mesmerised.

There she was on screen. Everything I wanted to be. I was only six and my future – or what I wanted my future to be – was standing right in front of me.

We were in the Hippodrome in Liverpool, a cinema in the heart of the city. Going to the pictures was a treat, and the occasion this time around was my birthday. I think it was 1960 and I was sitting next to our Frank and my mam. We were a film family and loved our trips to see the stars of the day. This time it was one of Hollywood's greatest movies of the era we were watching – Some Like It Hot.

My mum loved it. She was laughing away, tears rolling down her cheeks and my brother Frank was transfixed. They were engrossed by Tony Curtis and Jack Lemmon, putting in their now famous performance as two musicians on the run, escaping from the mob in an all-female band disguised as women.

But me? I only have eyes for Marilyn.

I am a glow...with Monroe.

She is everything a leading actress should be. Glamorous but with another side to her. She's playing Sugar Kane, but there's so much more to her than just a blonde.

'I wanna be loved by you, just you
Nobody else will do...'

"MARGI CLARKE – FIVE MINUTES"

The knock on the dressing room door brings me back to reality.

I'm on set in Manchester.

It's 50 years on from that day in the pictures. It's 2010 and I am doing what I am happiest doing. Working...acting.

At last I have made a breakthrough – finally at 56 I have become a grandmother – but only on telly. It's not the real thing, it's a role I'm playing in the primetime BBC drama about teenagers in a school called Waterloo Road.

I'm playing Bet, a battling granny, who ties herself to the railings in protest. See – still bolshie after all these years. I privately call my character Nana Ga Ga (that will catch on). I like playing this rebel with a cause because she has the makings of the little old granny I'll be.

But there's plenty more to be done before then...

I'll always remember back to when our Frank rang me when I was in Paris and said:

"Look, come home. You're Margi Clarke, not Petula Clarke.

"I've written a part for you."

But when I read the script I wanted to play Elaine, the romantic one in our Frank's movie.

I was going to play a chicken stuffer.

But our Frank said: "You've GOT to be her; she's the funny one and anyway, it all ends on your gob!"

It was one of the best decisions of my career.

Career. Now there's a word.

Well, you can now gatecrash mine.

The film delivered a big message to the world about Liverpool, its strength and refusal to crumble under what was a political attack from Thatcherism. When I look at the movie now, I see amazing things about the city that I find really touching. You forget, at that time, how still Liverpool was and how low the energy was.

There's a lovely scene where Elaine goes down to the river because she's heart sick for the love of her life. She looks out over the Mersey and not one thing goes up the river, not even a ferry. It was made at a time when we were at our lowest ebb but we were the big resistor, because we had such a massive spiritual strength.

We took it to Cannes. But, it was more than just one film and one festival – it was about selling the city to the world. We were like the Chamber of Commerce, because we were flying the flag. At that time Liverpool didn't even have a tourist office, never mind a film industry, and we were out there promoting it and saying how fantastic the city was. We wanted Liverpool to be the Hollywood of Britain and that's basically what happened. Brezhnev got a great reception everywhere we went and we won loads of awards, which was fantastic. We were living the high life – not in terms of money – but in experiences.

All the things I've been blessed with since, the tons of mad adventures which you will read about from Making Out, The Good Sex Guide to Coronation Street and so on. They have all stemmed from the beacon of Brezhnev. My mate Brezhnev, as I call it.

Well it's all here. The ups and downs, the ins and outs and, sorry, but got to go now – got a five-minute call.

Now you see me...

Alright, catch you at the end. I hope you've bought this book and aren't reading it in the shop.

Credits...roll...

Love, Margi x

'I used to send off my pocket money – when I could get it – to Avon for **freckle remover.** Thank God it never worked. So the story of the ugly duckling who turns into the swan is the pattern that I followed'

1. Postwoman Patsy

On the first day of primary school I walked there with my dad.

All the other kids were wailing and clinging on to their parents, and I dived straight into the sandpit. While they were all crying, I was made up to be making mud pies.

Both my elder sister and brother had been to Sacred Heart Roman Catholic Primary School in Kirkby ahead of me. Kathleen left and went to St Gregory's, the local Secondary school as I went into the Juniors.

What I recall most about that time is that I was always involved in sport. I was in the netball team. I was – and am – a typical Gemini. If you know your star signs you will know that Geminis have plenty of energy. That was me as a kid. Always running.

I usually played in two positions in the netball team. I was 'wing defence' but I also got a chance to play 'centre forward' – that was the best position because it meant that I could get everywhere. We'd go off on the bus to play other schools, so it was a big focus for me.

Even in the summer holidays, I'd go up on the school field and time myself running. I'd run in my bare feet.

I was always 'going on messages' for people – legging it everywhere and trying to beat my own little record. I set a long-jumping record at Sacred Heart that I think was unbroken until it closed a few years ago.

I started school in 1959. It was while I was at primary school that The Beatles happened. They were a big influence on me because it was when

Liverpool was opening out and making a statement to the rest of the world. They showed me that normal, young people from my city could go out and turn themselves into something special.

These four lads felt like brothers to us. It was also the start of my life-long love affair with John Lennon.

It was in the midst of Beatlemania gripping the planet that my sister Kathleen took ill. I was in the fourth year of the Juniors, aged 10. Kathleen was four years older than me.

She was ill for a long time, for 12 months. She had cancer. It was such a sad time for our family. While Liverpool the city was taking off, with people full of pride and joy at the success of John, Paul, George and Ringo and Bill Shankly's Liverpool Football Club, we were feeling so down. Our family was crying.

Kathleen loved The Beatles, but she also loved The Rolling Stones. One of the strong memories I have from that period was when my mam sent a letter to the Empire Theatre. She told them that Kathleen had terminal cancer, that she was only 15 and that she loved The Rolling Stones who were going to be playing there. Could they help out?

The good old Empire Theatre came up trumps. They gave her the box in the theatre. Kathleen went all dolled up – 60s style – and with all her friends and family including Sharon Patricia Maughan – the Kirkby-born, RADA-trained actress who was one of her very good friends. Sharon would go on to be the Nescafé Gold Blend woman in the adverts that were so big in the 80s and early 90s. It always made me laugh when I saw her years later on the telly talking as posh as posh can be. *To the Manor Born*...I don't think so. She was a Kirkby girl, just like me, with a strong imagination.

So they went to see The Stones and were hysterical – it was the first time that this brand new force of being a teenager had hit us. We had all these new ideas, and all our own clothes and we didn't look like our mams and dads. We were Thoroughly Modern Millies.

I was a very curious schoolgirl. I wanted to know the ins and outs of a whore's handbag. I'm still like that to this day – I'm itching to know. I was always on the go. I'm not happy till I know.

It was while I was in the Juniors that I began to recognise and get a peek on my future self. I did want to become a star. Oh yeah. It wasn't so much that I wanted the fame but I knew I had something.

Although good at English I didn't, ironically, have enough knowledge of words to articulate it...or understand it. But it was a driving force.

I wasn't particularly good at examinations. I didn't pass the 11-plus, which didn't disappoint me, but I was aware that there was a challenge that was going to stream you for your later educational life. For me it just meant that I would be going to St Gregory's where my sisters had already gone before me.

I was happy to be a Gregory's Girl going on messages, playing two balls and building dens. I had lots of friends. Leah was my best mate, and the youngest of a family of ten. Their house used to fascinate me because it was full of ornaments brought back by her father, who went away to sea. They had 36 lamps in the one house. They had dolls and all kinds of souvenirs and items from Japan. I was fascinated. It was a treasure trove.

I persuaded Leah to lend me an ornament to go on my mam's mantle piece, which was bare except for a 60s clock that had two painted ballerinas from Swan Lake on either side. I had to give the posey of flowers ornament back once Leah's mum had missed it.

Back in school, I wasn't a smart arse in the class, although I was the entertainer. On a Friday, I used to arrange for us to go and do the shows in front of the rest of the class.

I loved doing the latest pop song and acted out the words and did a 1965 song called Tossing and Turning by The Ivy League, with the lyrics: "I can't sleep at night tossing and turning." I was doing all the actions to that and The Searchers' classic Needles and Pins.

I wasn't rebellious – I was the leader of the class...the cock of the girls. I was just as vicious when it came to scrapping with the boys in our school. There used to be a kid who was terrified of me – Bobby Jenkins was his name – and he always used to ask my mother if I was in or if I was out so he could avoid me.

I was far more physical then, a bit like Pansy Potter – the Strongman's Daughter from the Beano, even though there was only two pence worth there of me. I wouldn't think twice about fronting something or someone, especially for my brother Frank. I certainly wasn't a bully – I wouldn't fight for myself, but if anyone touched our Frank, or one of the little kids, well, I'd roll my sleeves up and I'd be out there, on my toes, ready to 'glorm the gob' off someone.

Really, I was bright at school – that came out mainly through trying to write English essays. I had a great teacher called Mr Lavery in the fourth year. He was a history teacher, but he took other subjects too and I really enjoyed his classes.

Still, I got the strap at school. I can't remember what for – but we had the strap plenty of times. I was sent to the headmaster's office on one occasion. He was a nice old man, Mr Taylor. He smoked a pipe. I couldn't understand why this nice old fella was going to give me this punishment – the strap. I honestly can't recall what it was for, but I was always very talkative and distracted – probably some form of ADS – Attention Deficit Syndrome.

I don't remember what actually happened to my school reports. I never hid them. I always took them home. I don't think I was ever reported on 'badly'. But I left school at 15. I didn't have an 'O' Level to my name, but I loved the experience.

I suppose I got more attention at school than I did at home, because I came from such a big family, and I was right in the middle.

I loved having my own friends – extending my world. We did everything together – always an ensemble.

It left me with a strong craving for knowledge, information and the truth. It's got me into trouble sometimes, wanting to know the ins and outs of a cat's arse.

School really was the opening to that for me. That was where I started to really read. And I mean seriously read.

One of the teachers, Mr Bargery, was another favourite at St Gregory's and it was through him that I discovered books. He took care of the library. I love books, always have and always will.

When I was younger I didn't think I was very attractive. I had eyes like two 'No Entry' signs; a gob full of freckles; a heavy fringe – I looked like a muskrat. Squinting and saying: "Where d'yer go, where d'yer go?"

As far as I was concerned I didn't think I was remotely pretty, but my best friend, Leah, was very beautiful. Back then, I used to send off my pocket money – when I could get it – to Avon for freckle remover. Thank God it never worked. So the story of the ugly duckling who turns into the swan, is the pattern that I followed. It wasn't until I was about 18 that I got that first flowering, if you like.

Joey, a stud from Fazakerley, gamely sorted me out on the golf course by Aintree. Every time I watch the Grand National on the telly, I can see the golf course where nearly 40 years ago our arses bobbed up and down in unison.

After I left school at 15 (without a letter to my name) I got a start as an office junior at Fisher-Bendix, who make washing machines, and that was an incredible time. Sadly, like all the major companies that came to Kirkby aided by massive grants, they weren't there long enough before they asset-stripped their way out of the town leaving big employment gaps in the landscape. They took all the grants when they took over and set up, and then they pulled the rug on everything and everyone.

It was 1972. Workers' Solidarity was cracking in the air as the workers took over the factory for the first time. So I found myself bang in the middle of all that.

As my story unfolds that seems to be a recurring theme. I'm one of those people. I'm right there at the heart of things when a new cycle in life starts.

I'm like a catalytic converter – the blue touchpaper.

I've always been involved in bringing messages to the world like a Postman Pat.

First with Letter to Brezhnev announcing Perestroika.

Then with The Good Sex Guide – to be forewarned is to be fore-armed, and the Better Than Sex Vegetarian Cookbook, which came out just before we found out about BSE in the food chain.

So that's three good messages.

I've been part of delivering all my life...me, little Scouse me – Postwoman Patsy.

'When I look back
over my life, I feel like Lon
Chaney – you know, the
silent movie actor they called
"The Man Of A Thousand Faces."
That was me. So many
different faces'

2. Margi Loves Goliath

Looking back now my mam and dad, at that point, were still madly in love with each other while I was growing up.

Mam had a fantastic figure and gorgeous hair, and Dad was super fit, full of hardworking muscle – 'Iron Mick', that's what they called him. Dad was a former docker and then wagon driver. Mam worked for Littlewoods, but always had political fire in her blood.

They went out on a Saturday night – our Kathleen used to mind us and she – being the eldest – was like the little 'mother figure' while they went out to places like The Rising Sun pub on Dale Street – sadly, no longer there. They'd always have singsongs in the pub like those scenes depicted in Terence Davies films.

We'd have a singsong ourselves and we'd all be waiting up for them on a Saturday night.

We'd have a bag of crisps all evening – you know, the unready salted ones with the little blue salt bags in them. We'd be sat there in our knickers and vests – you didn't have pyjamas then, just a duvet cover or heavy blankets to keep you warm.

Mam and Dad would come back in after their night out, and the next day, the routine would be that we would dress in our 'Sunday Best' clothes and our little gang of Kirkby kids would visit both sets of grandparents in North Dingle in town. My Uncle Bernie and Grandma Barrett always gave us a tanner

We would be back on time for my dad's return from the Molly (The Molyneux), the local watering hole, where he'd been supping a 'Gilly ale'.

That was when we would have our homemade talent competitions. It's where it all started I suppose, performing for me mam on a Sunday afternoon.

We'd get up and belt out the songs on the kitchen table.

I was right in the middle of it – I loved those little shows. In my imagination I was on stage at the London Palladium. I was standing up there banging into Hello Dolly. "Hello Dolly...well hello Dolly". In my head I was there but instead of applause, Dad would fire a dishcloth at your gob.

We often had to make our own entertainment at home. We didn't have any books in our house at all and we had very few toys because there were that many of us – so we made up our own games. There's one that everyone played in Liverpool on all the estates – you know...boy/girl, animal/vegetable. It was our very own telly show.

Our real telly was broken. In those days you had to put money in the telly. I recall sitting on the back step filing halfpennies because we didn't have a shilling and the leccy would run out.

You would sit there filing it down so that it was the same size as a shilling. When the gas man turned up, my mother had to account for how many 'Kirkby shillings', as we called them, were in the meter. So we made up our own TV.

Another big part of Sundays was church. We'd get lashed out of the house and go up to church, and then after seeing the family, we had our roast dinner.

Then we were sent out to play again, whether we wanted to or not. I think it was then that my mam and dad were...making hay.

We used to go to the Sunday school around the corner at the Salvation Army.

I went there and was taught loads of religion, because they ran quizzes with religious questions and they gave sweets for the right answers. I was very good at answering religious questions – Margaret Mary Bernadette Clarke came into play then.

I still think about one question now. It was about David and Goliath.

They asked me about those two and I got it right because it was the bit where David kills Goliath.

Goliath doesn't see him – he's looking at something else, a sunset.

I thought: 'Well, that's not really the way of a Philistine, is it?'

Watching a sunset? I felt sorry for Goliath.

Anyway, I won a book...The Famous Five. I don't have that book now. I don't really have any momentos. I don't keep things. I didn't have very much, and what I did have I didn't keep because we all shared. It never worried me about sharing clothes, or anything.

It was the way it was. The way I am.

Our house was a big sharing wave – it started at the top and it rippled down to YOU.

I was asked once, what would I tell myself, as a child – if I could go back and meet the younger me? I think I would say that what you dream about – what you wish for yourself...can come true. We co-create the universe.

I always had a deep down understanding about myself that I was a distillation, if you like, of what my parents were and wanted to be. My mother was really intelligent, and my dad was also really bright, very strong, and had a lovely singing voice. He sang like a lark.

Throughout childhood, one of the most formative things was the culture we were brought up in.

We had lots of music – always playing Oklahoma, South Pacific, Seven Brides for Seven Brothers – and my family, like a lot of Scousers then, well, they were like the Hollywood victims. They really wanted to do it themselves. It was never going to be their generation that would actually do it – it would be the children of their generation.

So that was a strong education – about entertainment and stardom –

that came from the home.

That was what it was like then – everyone looked like a film star.

My mum looked like Joan Crawford and my dad looked like Robert Mitchum. As for me, my Uncle Teddy always said that I was the image of Katharine Hepburn.

That would have been the early Margi – the Margox.

When I look back over my life, I feel like Lon Chaney – you know, that was me. So many different faces.

I am just a girl who can't say...NO!

'I inherited her crucifix that was made for her, and it's the first thing I see when I wake up because it's right in the centre of my wall...those you lose become guiding spirits to you'

3. Our Kathleen

My sister Kathleen had a really big influence on my emotional life and my deep nostalgia for family.

We have a special date in our family that we've kept right through the decades all to ourselves, and that date is April 15th.

That was when Kathleen passed away but that was 1965, and it's also the same date 24 years later when the Hillsborough Disaster happened in 1989. That was the day when our Scouse brothers, sisters and fathers went off to a football match and didn't come back home. So it's become a tragic day for Liverpool.

Kathleen was the first 'star' in the family – she was beautiful – she was as dark as I'm fair and was the eldest sister. She looked like an Irish Colleen; she had lovely, clear skin, dark freckles and blue green eyes.

Kathleen was like our second mum, because although Mam was always there when we got up in the morning and when we went to bed, she was always busy – the classic Northern mother who had her sleeves rolled up...permanently.

My mother used to clean offices for solicitors when we were babies. We used to get taken to posh offices in Liverpool and be perched on a corner of the table while she scrubbed floors and polished telephones.

When Mam and Dad used to go out on a Saturday night out – that BIG Liverpool night out – Kathleen would look after us.

Me mam used to do her shopping early, usually with me in tow to

Kirkby market. Ham cobs were made on our return and the kettle went on, while Mum stood over the sink dyeing her hair. I used to watch her putting thick green mucky henna on to her hair, and I never thought it would turn out red. I was fascinated watching her transform.

Kathleen had a Saturday job in the market on the sweet stall. She wasn't one for giving away sweets or anything like that – she liked her job and she respected it too much. But she would bring home a load of sweets for the Saturday night.

I loved Butterkist popcorn and cream soda, and she'd get you that. Another favourite were Black Jacks sweets that made your tongue go nice and black, and we'd all get put in the bath. There'd be three of us in the one bath in our house in Didsbury Close, Kirkby.

My dad would lather us up and he said our Marrion used to "kill the soap" because she wouldn't lather up.

He said he only had to show me the soap and I'd be a mass of bubbles and I was the scruffy one – with a rip in my skirt, the ribbon in my hair askew and back to front and I'd have odd socks, one up and one down.

She was the eldest girl, a year younger than Michael, who was born when Mam was 19 and Dad was 17. My dad wasn't old enough to go to his own wedding party. My parents were married at that age and they had the 'do' in the Round House. Everyone was having a proper knees up in the pub, and my poor dad was sitting back home with my mother playing Ludo.

We were shipped out to Kirkby in 1959 from Sandhills and Kirkdale, where I was born. I was a north-end girl – from the north shore, where they used to sunbathe in regency days. There's something soft about the air there, and the light – it was like something Turner would have painted. The light was massively diffused as it left the river, which really left a lasting impression on me as a child. But Mam wanted to get away from the tenement we lived in – six kids on the top landing, no lifts and 92 stairs. I think the flat was only two bedrooms, and so Kirkby, to us, was the far off blue yonder hills. It was Beverly Hillbillies land Jed Clampett style, like the TV series, that we were getting taken to.

I was even aware, when I was small, that I was being dragged out of the heart of the city. It was still a fine Victorian town, packed with lots of shops and people, and we were being flung out into a field.

I totally looked up to our Kathleen – she was a brilliant sportswoman, and she won every competition she went in for. There was a cup dedicated to my sister at All Saints – which was called St Gregory's when we were there – because of her sporting achievements. She was naturally very graceful, but also had a bit of an autocratic personality.

She told us what to do and you did it. I loved her. She was naturally bossy, but I loved her. I don't think I was bossy as a kid – it was more about making yourself heard. There was always noise, and my dad says that's why I've got a big throttle – you develop a loud voice to be heard.

Kathleen had a beautiful voice, and she'd make us do talent competitions. I used to love watching her sing. She'd give so much passion to the song, she'd bring tears to her own eyes.

She was four years older than me, but I'm only very different to her in looks. I was like her in spirit and strength, I was sporty and competitive and I loved her sense of fashion – she was the first mod in the house. She was the one who had the nice clothes and I remember begging her to lend me this jumper to go to the Centre 63, which was our youth club. It was a really nice Italian mod jumper with four diamonds across the front of it, but it had bobbles of wool on it. Kathleen said I could lend the jumper if I picked all the bobbles off, which was a Herculean task.

She was into the growing soul scene. She used to go to the Rumbling Tum and she discovered the Sink Club, at the top of Hardman Street. She was quite rebellious in that she didn't have it big for The Beatles – as I've said, she loved The Stones much more.

When she was 15 she came in one day, about four o'clock from school, and said she was going to the doctors. I asked her: "What for, Kath?" and she said: "Does one of my legs look bigger than the other?"

I didn't notice but I was only 10 or 11. She went off to the doctors, and the medic – a lovely family doc called Doctor Healey – took one look at her and sent her straight to the hospital for tests.

Kathleen was doomed. There was nothing anyone could do for her. She was 15 and it took her 12 months to die – she fought like a tiger, and all that youthful dynamism fought this diagnosis of cancer. It was a sarcoma in her leg.

I always remember when Mam and Dad came back from the hospital months earlier. We were in the living room and they were in the back kitchen – Kathleen had been kept in the hospital.

They put the mop pole under the door so we couldn't get in, and they were crying. I'd never heard both of my parents cry. We were banging on the door, we didn't know what was happening, but the mop pole stopped us getting in.

We weren't told she was dying. We didn't know.

Liverpool was playing out on the world's stage with The Beatles, and all that happiness that they brought passed us by. We were crying while everyone else was laughing and celebrating. So, although consciously you didn't know exactly what was going on, subconsciously you were very aware of WHAT was happening.

We were told what Kathleen was told – that she had an abscess on her leg. It was said that she would be alright when the abscess burst.

On the day she died – it was a week or so after Easter – I selfishly thought: "Who's going to get all our Kathleen's Easter eggs?"

I didn't realise what death meant.

Part of her distilled into me – the part that wanted to be a star. I followed that path after watching her singing. She was a fantastic dancer. There's still quite a bit of Kathleen that will be forever with me.

Loss is long term, isn't it? Although Shakespeare said: "Nothing's lost" – that's one line I love out of the Bard.

But grief is a long-term thing.

I used to be called a hero when I was a kid and I used to love hearing it. If I did anything courageous or outrageous, I'd hear it. I think, when

Kathleen died, I took some of her hopes and ambitions on board. I can't remember many of the conversations we had, but I recall the feelings.

She was protective of us all. She had to look after us, as a second mother, because Mam had a job and Mam would be going to work as Kathleen came home from school. So Kathleen would put the tea on.

But it was the Saturday night when she really came into her own as Mum Number Two, after we'd had our hair gone through with the steel nit comb – I used to hate that. That's when she took over.

You don't ever know how much your memory is embellished but if you've had a big family, there's always triumph and tragedy.

You're not aware of that when you're growing up, you don't realise that the odds are that these things are going to happen. If you've lived through that, it's like a nuclear bomb going off in your family.

It's the worst form of poverty.

Poverty in your pocket can always be rectified and re-filled, but to have had the loss of someone so young and beautiful and full of every bit of the potential that I was full of – it was what melded us all together afterwards.

I didn't just lose my sister. I lost my brother ten years later from a motorbike crash, so all my pain from Kathleen onwards, all goes back to that first agony of losing her.

When I lost her I remember promising her that I'd never forget her, and I'd never let her down. And I took that literally at the beginning, and up until I was 16 I religiously went to the cemetery. Even when there was a bus strike one year, I walked from Kirkby to West Derby – where she's buried – because I was devoted to her.

I still commune with her every day – I inherited her cross that was made for her, and it's the first thing I see when I wake up because it's right in the centre of my wall.

So it's continuous – past and future, are in the now.

And those you lose become guiding spirits ever more.

'When I was 17
I begged my mum to be a
belly dancer . . .
I'd read all about the rich
sheiks and I thought "I'll go to
Beirut and I'll cop off
with one"'

4. Just the Job…

At 15 I took on the big world outside.

My first job came courtesy of a Merseyside Institution – the Football Pools.

I really wanted to go to Littlewoods Pools because that was where my older sister Marion and all her mates were – my mother herself had worked there as an 18-year-old – and they really looked after you. It was a very paternal company.

They used to take the whole work away on summer trips, like to Blackpool which was my favourite, and we'd all be at Lime Street, all dolled up, and the train would be waiting for us to take us to this great resort with its own 'Tower Power'.

I was at Littlewoods for about two years, up until I was about 17. It was strict, but I was used to all that because I'd been to St Gregory's, which was run by the nuns. Littlewoods Pools was like St Gregory's in that it was all women. There were a few men who worked in security and a few who repaired things, but that was it – a Queenie domain.

Littlewoods was great, with all those women that worked there, and all the opportunities that they took you on – you got sent to the hairdressers once a year for free. They really looked after everyone. It was owned by the Moores family, Aristo-Liverpudlians who go way back in Liverpool's history.

Master Simon Moores used to come around checking on the staff, and he was really dishy. He was always called Master, never Mister. You had to put your hand up to go to the toilet for a ciggie. It was like being back in school in a way: "Please, Sir, Miss, can I, er, go for, er..."

If you were longer than three minutes the whole pool knew you'd been putting false eyelashes on.

We were always buying stuff out of the Littlewoods catalogue. I remember ordering this red spotted bikini and me and my mate Jane Hodder were skivin' in the toilet trying on the bikinis, and for a laugh I hooked her up onto the back of the door, with her bikini bra – she was even smaller than me. We got caught and there was murder. I got sent to personnel.

If you felt ill – I remember fainting once, and because it was all open plan, everyone could see – out came this massive old Victorian bath chair. I got put in it and pushed through the building. I could see through a cocked eye they were all laughing at me. I have a bit of low blood pressure – it's naturally low. So if it goes too low, maybe I haven't had enough to eat or something, then I might faint, which is how I ended up in the bath chair on my way to the sick bay.

After Littlewoods, I got a job as a barmaid in the evening, at the British Legion in Kirkby. I've always been flighty and a bit of a bolter. Jobs were ten a penny.

I had all kinds of what my mother called 'crackpot ideas'. When I was 17 I remember once begging my mum if I could go to belly dance in Beirut. At this time Frank was working with Paul O'Grady – Lily Savage – as a barman at a Masonic lodge.

I've always been a reader – always enjoyed reading, but we didn't have many books in our house. I'd read about all the sheiks in London, and all the dolly birds copping off with them, and I thought, 'I'll go to Beirut and I'll cop off with a sheik.'

I had a strawberry blonde Afro wig, and nipped in velvet trousers, and false eyelashes top and bottom – my eyes were that heavy with make-up, they looked like no entry signs, or a cross between Ghengis Khan and Björk.

I liked to be out there with the crowd and I was born to be sociable. I needed to grow up fast and make my own money. I wanted an adult life, so I fiddled my age and got the job as a barmaid. I was 17 by then.

I'd left Littlewoods when I stumbled upon another job. It was with Leatherbarrow's, the building firm. I met the boss's wife, Mrs Leatherbarrow, when I was working at the Legion and she took a shine to me. She wanted to turn me into a lady, and used to take me for cups of tea in George Henry Lee – the famous old department store in the centre. Now it's John Lewis in the multi-million pound shopping precinct Liverpool One. Time moves us all on.

I must have been dead cheeky, but I ended up working for Leatherbarrow's as a receptionist. I still kept on the Legion job, too. I didn't get tired – it didn't take a feather out of me.

I left Leatherbarrow's after there was a strike, and went to work on the Dock Road as a telephonist for Davis and Timmins, who are mentioned in Letter to Brezhnev. They made industrial screws of all shapes and sizes. It really suited what some of my inner dreams were about.

I didn't tell my mother that I had left Leatherbarrow's, and I managed to get the bus into town – to Vauxhall Road – without her knowing. I'd arranged it that if she rang they were to say that I'd just gone out for a cup of tea or something. I just didn't want to tell her that I'd left yet another job.

It was always low wages – less than if I'd worked in a factory because you got overtime if you worked in a factory. I was still earning money as a barmaid, which my mother did know about. And in between jobs I was working at the envelope factory – Dickinson's. Now that was hard work.

I didn't last long there – I think I only did about six months. My sister, Eileen, worked there for years and she loved it, but it was tough work. You had to run a machine that was as big as a ship – it was massive. It was always essential to get another job before my mother found out that I'd left the previous one. I always found one because I was always very enthusiastic, I looked fab and I had the gift of the gab. And there was always a lot of work available then.

I picked up lots of skills along the way. For example, I taught myself how to become a telephonist. I'd said I could do it to get the job – it was an old fashioned plug board, one step up from the one Granny Clampett uses in The Beverly Hillbillies with a long extended wire on it. You had maybe 10 or 20 phone lines, each one of them had a lead that you pulled out from a rest, where all the lines rested and you placed it across into a channel.

So, you could get your mates ringing up and you could plug them into a call in Australia. I loved it because it was about communicating, and I always liked using my voice. I wasn't aware then, that that was what I liked – you're not that aware about yourself then. It's only when you look back that you can see those traits developing in you.

Telephonists were the first port of call at the company and you were presenting a character. So it was about being clear and having nice diction, so it was like a first little acting job – my first line was: "Good morning, Davis and Timmins, can I help you, can I put you through?" That was the first little opening.

All these roles are like archetypal parts for Northern women. I'd also worked for a bedding factory – Downham Bedding up on the estate – where they stuffed pillows. It was the craziest place I'd worked in all my days. It was a factory but I got a job in the office. It had terrible working practices – there was no health and safety. God knows how it was allowed to be open. There was a big hole in the roof that you could have put an elephant through, over where people were making the beds, stapling the wooden frames – and this was in the middle of winter.

The canteen was just a little hut, and at the back of the hut was a little stove. When I asked what that was for, I was told that was where you could stand your can of soup. You put your can of soup, with about 15 others' cans of soup, with the lids open, in this little oven.

I was once told that I'd had about nine thousand, nine hundred and ninety-nine lives, and my career's been a bit similar, with all that diversity. You've got to adapt or die, haven't you? It's about survival, which is marked within Liverpool people's character as well – we don't give in easy.

We're at our strongest when we're at our lowest ebb because that's when we transform and come back. Brezhnev reflects that. It basically told of the time, and the time then in Liverpool during the 80s was at its most still. The river was empty, and there was no work for anyone.

It was at its quietest.

I attracted boyfriends – I attracted a whopper in the betting shop and that was Joey. He was one of those who wouldn't pay the tax, and I really liked him because he was dead cheeky himself.

He was a bit of a gadfly. He was proper fit – he was tall and he looked a bit Mexican because he had a Zappata moustache. He looked a bit like Jimmy Hill actually because he had a big chin. He asked me out – I worked in the pub where he lived in Fazakerley, in the Copple House.

I'd skitted around loads of pubs – I was at The Chaser by Fazakerley station, The Carter's Arms in Kirkby and The Slaughter House in town. I got a fright one night when a boyfriend came in gang-handed and ordered pints and doubles all round, then when it came to pay he sent me to the till with a bottle top in my hand.

I thought, 'What am I going to do with this bottle top?' and I lashed it over my shoulder, and started serving someone else. We were canny lassies then. We didn't ever want to rob the manager of his stock because that wouldn't be fair.

You wouldn't last very long in the job, but we used to sell our own booze. We put our own whisky up in the optics. You'd fiddle a few bob, but the stock wouldn't be down because we'd top up the optics with cheap whisky. That was an old trick of the trade. It's probably impossible to do that now because everything's camera-ed up, and the tills are just not adding up – are they?

Joey asked me out, but when you went out with Joey you sort of went out with all his mates because he always went about in a gang. I lost my virginity to him one lovely summer's night.

I think I was just 18 – it would have been after my birthday in May. I used to have this long maxi skirt with laurel print on it, and a big handbag that looked like a horse's hay bag.

I had my Afro wig on and my false eyelashes. My dad used to hate me wearing that honey-coloured Afro wig. He'd drag it off my head and lift up an old mat we had by the door with all dead grass under it, and he'd say: "That's what your hair's going to be like." And he'd have a big soapy flannel in his hand, which he'd throw at me to get the makeup off. I had to be home by midnight, because all the rest of the girls were still at home so I couldn't be leading the way, and he was quite strict. He worked on the lorries then, and he'd be up early in the morning.

He always wanted you home early, and of course I wouldn't want to go in. I'd only just got going. You'd come out of the pub and there was nowhere open after half 10 in Kirkby, and so the next thing I'm trying to get into the house at about five o'clock in the morning, having been with Joey on Fazakerley Golf Course, in a bunker. Losing my virginity wasn't a magical experience. It was premeditated – I knew it was coming, and I'd brought a blanket with me in my handbag.

I was with Joey for about a year before he went with someone else, who was a posh librarian. And then I met Billy in the local watering hole, The Woodpecker, in Kirkby.

I wasn't working there – I was a customer. Everyone was smoking pot in there, it was quite free and easy. I started smoking at about 18. I've never been into drink in a big way, but I've always enjoyed my smoke.

Billy used to sit up in The Woodpecker and he looked like David Bowie. He was the thin white duke. He was blond, tall and slim.

He was really hardy and very, very strong with sinewy powerful muscles. He had his own little haulage company with a couple of wagons, with his dad. We copped off together and I sort of knew it was serious. We got together quite quickly and my mother didn't want me to go off with him. She wanted me to stay with my studies, because I went to Elliot Clarke's (Theatre School & College) in 1972 after St Gregory's. Then I got pregnant, after I'd been with Billy for three years. I got married in 1973 when I was 19 and I had our Laurence in 1976.

My mam and dad didn't turn up at the wedding because a) they didn't believe me and b) it was Christmas Eve – my mother's busiest day of the year.

It was also the foggiest, iciest day on record, and it sent everything up the pole. So we had to get two strangers from the rent office. I got my wedding dress from Silly Billy's in Whitechapel – a fabulous hippy shop – owned by Carla Lane's sons, Carl and Nigel.

Billy went on to set up rehearsal and recording studios in Manchester Street – he had the Ministry of Love at the time of punk. When we got married I enacted being a housewife in my head, but I was so bad at being a housewife in reality that I flooded the house out twice.

I must have been on the ducking stool in a previous life. I was like a canary in a gilded cage. It was a bit like Educating Rita – I wanted to go off and see the big world. I was beginning to develop an interest in show business. Billy's a really private person – we were like chalk and cheese – we were completely different. But Billy's my first love – we fell in love listening to Lou Reed's Perfect Day, and we used to be blissfully happy driving in his Ford Zeffa car up to Ainsdale and going to the beach.

Me and Billy are really good friends now. I left him in 1979 when I met another lad. He was called Jamie Reid, after I'd started to get into music that would eventually lead to me becoming Margox.

'I wanted to get out
and be part of the
creative scene and the
first place I had to conquer was
my home city. It still is.
Punk was the
big liberator.
I'd done poetry gigs and I
thought: "Right, now I'll put it
to music"'

5. Margox

It was a great time to be growing up in Liverpool in the late 1970s. Punk had arrived. As soon as I heard about this new cultural explosion I knew I had to – wanted to – be part of it. I was.

So I got a band together and called it Margox and the Zinc.

The Zinc part of the band name came about because my sister Kathleen used to go to The Sink Club at the top of Hardman Street in Liverpool during the sixties. Everyone from the south end of the city went there and my sister Kathleen used to go there with her friends. She told me that you got in free if you brought a bath or sink plug along. All my mam's plugs went missing.

At the time, though, I didn't realise it was called The Sink Club – I thought it was Zinc. So that explains one half of the band name but people always ask me – where did the name Margox come from?

Well, when I was looking at a glamour picture of Margaux Hemingway in Vogue magazine I said to our Frank: "Isn't that 'Margox' Hemingway gorgeous looking?"

He said: "Yes, she is gorgeous – but you don't pronounce the X."

Well, of course, as far as punk went, anything with an x was considered to be where it was at...The Sex Pistols and Siouxsie and the Banshees to name just two.

It was avant garde, bringing a letter in the English language that we didn't use very much into common usage.

So there it was, up for grabs, and I became Margox.

It was such an unusual name...although every witch in folklore history is called Morgana or Margaret, you know. But not every Margaret is a witch.

It was a pure creative mistake, and I was made up with how cool it sounded. I had already been playing with my name – I was Margaret, I was Margi, then I wanted to be Maggie, but I'd been warned off Maggie because I'd been told by my grandmother Clarke that it was a prostitute's name. They had the old seventy-eight (78 not a 45) of Maggie May, and I've always been fascinated by that character. We used to play it as kids – it used to have on the record 'by persons/author unknown' – and we'd roar laughing at its uniqueness. It reminded me of all the old ninnies, and that Georgian/Victorian Liverpool, so I'd always been tuned into the Maggie scenario. It was a Maggie connection that fascinated me and, years later, still frequently makes me smile.

When we hit our 'creative mistake' we roared laughing at it. It was just like the time I said to our Frank, my brother, that Jayne Casey, a leading light in the punk movement, was 'weirder than me.'

Frank said: "No kid, she just looks weird – you are weird."

I took that as a marvellous compliment.

When I became Margox, I hoped to become a singing sensation. I'd always wanted to be recognised as a singer but before that came the poetry.

I'd written some stuff and Adrian Henri, Brian Patten and Roger McGough – The Mersey Sound Poets – had included some of my work on their tour.

My elder brother Michael loved Adrian Henri and the adventures of the Beat Poets because it reminded him of the American poet Allen Ginsberg and a journal called The Howl, and that whole beatnik side.

It all took off when I went along to O'Connor's Tavern on Hardman Street and chatted up Adrian Henri after he got me a glass of cider. And then Willie Osuo tried to sell me a tab of acid – everyone from the south end knew Willie – though he's passed away now. He had a massive Afro hairstyle.

There I was, having walked into the bar on my own. I was always taking risks going to places on my own – testing out how strong my sense of being an independent woman was.

I used to go to all kinds of clubs – little dives in back alleys, all on my own. Traces of that independence go back to my childhood when I was eight and I was covered in warts – I've still got one on my finger now. I had a terrible complex because no one ever wanted to hold my hand. I thought I was really ugly and I used to get the piss taken out of me. I had to go to Belmont Road Hospital and I used to take myself on the bus to the Outpatients department – warts and all. I'd go off on my own and have them painfully burnt off because I was so embarrassed about the way they made me look.

Around that time, I also used to go and visit my grandmother who lived in town. I'd go on the bus and travel the nine miles alone constantly gazing out the window in the hope of not paying my bus fare to the conductor. I always had that sense of freedom and independence.

Anyway, I'd written these poems and Adrian Henri got me to go on stage at the Everyman Theatre. That was the first step to getting the band together.

I probably did have a subconscious drive – an attraction to make connections with people where I could show what I could do and express myself. I went direct to Adrian, and at the same time I connected to Allan Williams of Beatles fame – when I met him in a nightclub and danced to David Bowie's The Man Who Sold The World for him.

He said I had 'something' and I told him I wanted to be a singer, but I didn't tell him that I couldn't sing at this point. He took me to this opera singer in town, who taught me the basic rules.

Adrian and Allan were on the steps to Margox – I was testing people's reaction to ME.

I felt I could magnetise people towards me. I had something. I had that confidence – I'd been trained in that by Mam and Dad – all the singing, all the dancing and all the political background we'd been reared with.

I definitely had self-belief and I was already beginning to read about Liverpool's culture, and became interested in what was happening in the city. I was just drawn towards it.

My poetry was all, "who am I, where am I going" – with a bit of a punk attitude. My hair wasn't Margox Red at this point.

I was my natural auburn, but I was switched on. I was full of myself like most young people but I was kept in natural check because I was a Kirkby girl. My accent always stopped me getting above myself. I was in people's faces, I was so full of life and energy – self-assured, that's what was aggressive about me. I play aggressive – it's that intensity that we have in this city – it's how others see me. So I knew I had something different but I was more vain about my brain. Again, I'd gained a confidence over time that I'd developed since I was at school.

Part of that determination was borne through overcoming disappointment earlier in life. It used to upset me that I never got picked for some things. At school I so wanted to join the Morris Dancing team – I used to sit on the back step and cut up the Liverpool Echo into strips and sew them into pompoms. But I never got picked by the teachers – maybe because my hands were covered in newsprint! Yet, I knew I was good enough.

I longed to be out there, but I was living the same life as everyone else around me and could only dream. Reality hit home and I had to go and get myself a job at 15. I didn't go to college, although I did actually go back to St Gregory's when I was 18 and got an O' Level in pottery. Amazingly, the pottery I made during that time became the communion chalice for the nuns at Sacred Heart.

But I wanted to get out and be part of the creative scene and the first place I had to conquer was my home city.

It still is. I haven't conquered it yet – it's still the toughest. I haven't done that many shows in Liverpool.

Punk was the big liberator. I'd done poetry gigs with Roger McGough, and I knew I had to write some more, but I didn't really have the inspiration and I didn't want to get up and do the same set again. I thought 'right, ok, I'll put it to music'.

That's what gave me the idea to get a band. It was then that I met the famous musical entrepreneur Roger Eagle, who was such an inspiration to so many bands and musicians in Liverpool.

I went to the old Liverpool Stadium – which used to be right by where we filmed that scene in Letter to Brezhnev by the tunnel. Sadly, the famous arena was knocked down in 1982. It was where all the unions met, boxing matches went on and obscure bands played.

I went there to see Roger's band called Can – the first prototype electronic band. Roger used to sit up in a box at the side, on stage with a girl called Doreen. I used to look up and think I'd love to meet them. He was a big fella who used to wear a Stetson hat. Roger was a big character. He wasn't from Liverpool – I didn't know that then.

Anyway, there he was one day, sitting in the Kardomah cafe, which was a place that was popular with the movers and shakers in Liverpool. I used to love going there, because you'd always find someone you knew, or wanted to know. You'd see the world and its mother going past. Roger was sitting in the bubble part of the window and so I go up and slim myself into the seat next to him and start chatting him up.

He said to me: "What music d'you like?"

I told him that I loved Captain Beefheart and that I loved Can.

He was really impressed, because if you liked them it was like having a membership to the club.

He asked me what I did and I said I was a singer. That was a little tactic that I used, when I look back now. I used to say I was an actor when I'd never acted and a singer when I never sang. It was like a sympathetic magic, you know?

If you pretend it, you become it. But Roger called me out on it and he said: "Oh, have you got a band?" And I said: "Yeah, Margox and the

Zinc." I had the title of the band but I didn't tell him I didn't actually have the members of the band. A month later he gave me a gig at Eric's. That was a start.

If you'd got a chance there then it could be the beginning of something.

Everybody in Liverpool and in the national music scene knew about Eric's. OMD, Teardrop Explodes, Elvis Costello, Wah! and ME – we all played there.

It lasted from 1976 to 1980. Now there is a musical written about it.

But just as I got my first big break in music, little did I know that my life was about to change again.

At the time, I was living on the top landing of a Kirkby tower block – married to Billy with our Laurence – then only a baby. It was a Saturday and we'd had a terrible fight that morning. I can't remember what it was about – but I was crying.

Then there was a knock on the door.

When I opened it, there was a family friend to tell me that "Michael was dead."

Michael was my brother and he had been killed on a motorbike.

Although you accept in a big family that there will be triumph and tragedy, well, I'll never forget that day. When I was younger I had to deal with Kathleen's death. Now it happened again – same family.

Two weeks before that I had dreamt my brother's death.

I think I'm just extra sensitive. Sometimes I get the shadow of events – just before. Time isn't linear is it? Time does its own thing. In the Celtic tradition you had Banshees and Seers, and they didn't come back with visions of a land of milk and honey, they were the protectors of the tribe by seeing the shadows of events yet to come.

This was all what was going on before I became famous as Margox. Just like after Kathleen's death, I had to get on with things after Michael died.

I started to build up a reputation in the city, which began with the very first publicity anyone did for me. London-born, Liverpool-based critic Philip Key wrote about me in the Daily Post, when I'd done the poetry and he referred to my "sparkling Irish eyes".

I was doing a showcase at Kirklands nightclub and I'd jumped on a table at the club as part of the performance – I used to do spontaneous things like that. It helped me get noticed.

I could have forged ahead with Margox and the Zinc, but one of our main band members – Drew Schofield – went into acting in a production of Of Mice and Men. It worked well for him. He put in a really powerful performance and it turned out to be the start of a successful career for him. He went on to great things, working with Alan Bleasdale and he has become one of the most respected actors from the area. Most people know him as Andrew Schofield but to us he'll always be Drew.

Me and Drew were very competitive with each other. I'd got the band together, having been galvanised into action by Roger who had given me a date – a deadline to get things up and running by.

I found Drew's brother Glen first, who was a fantastic drummer.

So in the beginning it was me and a drummer.

Then we got Drew in and Paul Pilnock, who used to play with Steeler's Wheel plus Caroline Jones – a brilliant flautist.

This was Margox and the Zinc. It was quite jazzy.

Drew was into Santana, the latin rock band – but I hated them and used to call them Sultanas. I didn't want the band to be quite so jazzy. What I did with it was really avant garde, turning this poetry I had into songs.

One song was about custard slices. My dad used to have two custard slices every day and two Sayers pies, and this was in homage to him.

Just before our first gig at Eric's, I met film director Chris Bernard at the Liverpool School of Language, Music, Dream and Pun at Ann Twackey's, which was another one of those 'happening' places in the city.

That school was such an amazing experience for about 500 people in

Liverpool then. It was all centred around Mathew Street.

That simple thoroughfare has had such an amazing pull to creative people over the decades.

It's on a major ley line – I think Bill Drummond connected it to Iceland.

Chris and I got on like a house on fire – our families had known each other for years – and he has such an artistic flair. He was into theatre and was involved with the late Ken Campbell. Ken had come up to do Illuminatus, part of which was staged at the language school.

Anyway, for my first gig, Chris made me this cloak – like a Bela Lugosi cape – black with a big standee-up collar, which I wore years later when I played the wicked witch in Snow White.

And that was what I wore for my very first appearance at Eric's.

I remember getting ready for that gig. I was really nervous because I knew that all the people that I looked up to were all going to be there: Pete Burns, Holly Johnson, Jayne Casey – they were all in that crowd. Making a good impression on them meant more to me than anything. I was an old punk – I was 22 – and I was THE oldest punk.

The roof went off and it was a fantastic debut performance – I couldn't have done it any better even if I was doing it now with all the skills I've learnt. It was like the cork coming out of the bottle. I was gabbing loads to the audience, telling them how I'd bunked the bus to get there, and all sorts of funnies.

At one point I kicked my stilettos off – I had a little basque on when the cloak came off. I was having a bit of a Judy Garland moment, and I was giving it everything. Then I saw our Frank in the audience mouthing the words: "Turn around kid," and when I turned around Drew was busy upstaging me playing his guitar with my stiletto.

That was the birth of Margox. That's where it all started and it was at Eric's being Margox that I got my next break.

Later on, after that first performance, Anthony H Wilson came along to the club and saw me. Manchester and Liverpool, then, were really close – the music brought us all together.

Before that, everyone used to go up to The Wheel over there, and Tony Wilson – as he was better known – was involved with Roger Eagle and Pete Fulwell, and he brought his Factory Records acts over to Eric's.

I was playing that night. I was opening for Adam and the Ants, and Tony came across for what was my first professional performance on stage. I think he spotted me because I was very visual, and had lots of patter. I worked off the crowd and was pretty outrageous at the time.

Some weeks after that, Drew had left me with a dilemma because he'd bailed out to pursue acting. Billy and I were living in Arkwright Street – Margaret Mary Bernadette in Orange Lodge area – and then I got a phone call...from Tony Wilson's producer at Granada.

Tony was kind.

He was moving on but he spotted something different – he was sweet and lovely, a generous man and I miss him.

So I got the job. I was a presenter on the regional What's On show called er, What's On.

I enjoyed 12 months on the telly and it made Margox into a name, a face.

It was regional – but for half-an-hour every Friday I butted in and out.

I got up to all sorts in the name of local arts. When it was over, I moved on but it was the best grounding ever for me and what lay ahead.

Probably my most embarrassing moment ever recorded on tape is languishing somewhere in a vault in Granada TV Studios. It was regarded as too OTT for It'll be All Right on the Night to show...

It features me wetting myself on a trampoline.

My producers Geoff Moore and the famous David Liddiment – weeks earlier – sounded me out on the idea of bringing in a world expert trampolinist to put me through acrobatic twists and jumps on the said contraption.

When Geoff told me there would be no rehearsal, the camera turned on me the minute I bounced on the rubber.

I guessed they were after an amateur, ungraceful performance, but unbeknown to the team I had won a bronze medal at the Centre 63 Youth Club for trampolining.

So I thought, "Right, I'll show them."

I turned up on the day of filming wearing a really tight-fitting, purple cat suit.

I didn't want to spoil the effect of a visible panty line ruining the 'painted on' cat suit look so I left my knickers off – big mistake.

My plan was to spring into action, hauled on by the world expert in the field of trampolining.

I dived 20 feet into the air and executed a fine pike straddle but I'd thrown my legs open with such force that a big blast of piss shot clean out of my cat suit.

For some reason, it's not showable, that one.

Anyway, apart from that, What's On was great for me. I didn't realise it at the time, but it unlocked a lot of telly doors. Miss yer, Tony.

'Poplar trees swayed together
like married couples in
the train's drift stream.
Little white houses
with red-tiled roofs and
shuttered windows sped
endlessly by. Paris. I'd never
been abroad before'

The Clarke clan at my Aunty Kathleen's wedding.
Can you spot me...I'm the one in front of my father,
the one with the halo. Eyes like No Entry signs...

Blackler's Grotto in 1958. I'm
at the back, then Marion,
Kathleen and our hooded Frank

Before tragedy strikes: Mum with
Michael, aged two-and-a-half and
Kathleen, then nine months, in 1951

Intensity and Passion!

My first publicity shot in the '70s for the Liverpool Echo

Into the '80s, with my soul lover artist Jamie Reid at the height of our passion. The image became the cover of our record Beauty and the Thief on French Polydor

Brezhnev Babes!

Me and Alexandra Pigg enjoying success in our home town on the steps of the Adelphi Hotel

Alexandra and Peter Firth had on-screen chemistry. They sizzled as lovers Elaine and Peter in an iconic scene image from *Letter to Brezhnev*

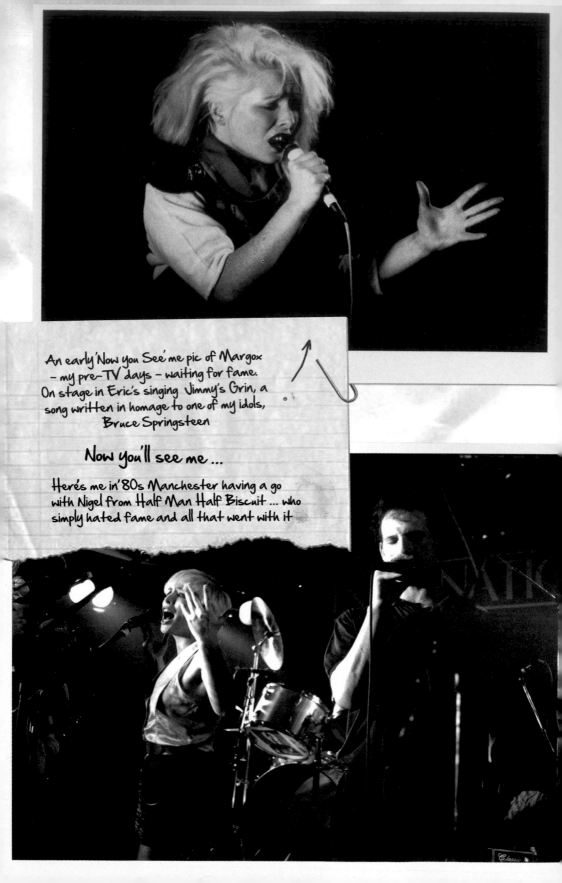

An early 'Now you See' me pic of Margox
– my pre-TV days – waiting for fame.
On stage in Eric's singing Jimmy's Grin, a
song written in homage to one of my idols,
Bruce Springsteen

Now you'll see me ...

Here's me in '80s Manchester having a go
with Nigel from Half Man Half Biscuit ... who
simply hated fame and all that went with it

The Fab Three. Alexandra, George Harrison and me at an award ceremony at the Savoy London. One of my all-time favourite pics

Oh boyu!

Leek to the press, in 1987. Backed by Welsh band Yr Anhrefn, whose Rhys Moyen co-wrote with me Clutter from the Cut ler. It made the top 10 of the Welsh charts!

Making Magic

Oh what a happy cast on the first day of the series Making Out, in 1989. Ring-leader Keith Allen (whatever happened to him?) in the middle of a bunch of the finest women actors of the era. The factory females were: Rachel Davis, Heather Tobias, Me, Tracie Bennett, Shirley Stelox, Moya Brady and Melanie Kilburn

In the arms of able-bodied seamen, who were on a visit to the Mersey River Festival in 1989

Queenie showing some leg. What a great time me and the cast spent in 'Manny'... better known as 'Madchester'

Carry on Cleopatra

It beats keeping coal in the bath! This was a chocolate advert for Options hot choc drink in 1995. It focused on sensual indulgence and you can't say Pharaoh than that. This was my first commercial. I also became Bixie in a Weetabix ad!

Ronnie O'Dowd and the big K.O. She punched for girls everywhere back in 1991

Going all arty, starring in one of a trilogy of European films after Brezhnev

I don't 'arf like this fella on the left. A Good Sex Guide episode about a 1994 survey on how size doesn't matter. Didn't these rugby players scrub up well!

6. Paris & London

It started with that timeless routine of getting ready for a good Saturday night, and as most girls know the best part is in the excited preparation.

That moody Saturday afternoon in the late 1970s, when I remember Liverpool playing a friendly at home to Celtic, proved to be a win for Liverpool and as it turned out...a win on a soul level for me.

I put the spuds on a low light and while the pot cooked, started the beauty regime which involved bolting 33 old-fashioned perming rollers tight to my scalp to achieve the look of my distinctive red hair. Pain had to be endured to get a tight curl for the back-combed style that would crown my entrance that night at Eric's.

I was distracted by a knock at the front door downstairs on the ground floor below. Without a scrap of make-up on and a head full of Nora Batty metal I didn't paint a pretty picture. I know it's hard to believe.

I yanked open the rattling sash window and flew my head out like I'd done a million times before and there...staring up at me from the street was my secret hero, Jamie Reid.

He was the man whose face I'd been looking at only weeks previously, pictured scowling (it wasn't the done thing to be caught posing with a smile on your gob in punk days) with a serious Malcolm McLaren in the Rock and Roll magazine NME. He was the designer who had been influential in giving the Sex Pistols their distinctive look.

Back when I looked upon the magazine picture I didn't guess for a minute that any day soon the man from the capital would be looking up at ME knocking on my door.

It was HIM that cut the pretty unforgettable picture. His black glossy hair swept back like Al Pacino caught the light. He was decked out in Vivienne Westwood gear with an oil-skinned teddy boy frock coat, trimmed in kinky, black rubber button collar and cuffs. His Doc Martin boots were a different shade of ox blood.

My heart raced as I looked at him and I fell in love at first sight.

His surprise visit had been arranged by our mutual good friend – Jon Savage.

Jon was an excellent, astute Zeitgeist writer, summing up in words the culture shock that was happening around our ears. He was right there at The Sex Pistols' first-ever gig and a champion and archivist of Jamie's work, going back to his first agi-pop images and world shattering Sex Pistols art work. Jon later went on to write the definitive punk history book 'England's Dreaming', and he had worked with me as a producer on Margox/What's On.

Although he was dead posh, he was a true punk anarchist and acted in the background, mentioning me to Jamie as our paramour.

It was the real thing between me and Jamie.

But I was torn...

Jamie wanted me to go to Paris but I knew that would mean leaving Laurence behind. Looking back, making the decision to go was the most awful thing I ever did.

I was right not to take my son with me, and subject him to the life me and Jamie had over there. His father has a great relationship with Laurence, he's always provided stability in his life. Meeting him was one of the better judgements in my life. I still did a runner at the end of the day and I regret that. We have a great relationship now – you can't get closer. I'm really proud of my lad.

It was just a couple of weeks after meeting Jamie that our bags were packed and we bolted to Paris. It was the start of a great 16-year adventure...which still goes on in my head. On a mild January afternoon we arrived in Calais after a long journey across the Channel, to a fast train through the French countryside and on to Paris!

Poplar trees swayed together like married couples in the train's drift stream, as little white houses with red-tiled roofs and shuttered windows sped endlessly by. I'd never been abroad before and reflected.

Here I was on my way to live and take my chance in a foreign city, when I'd only been to London a couple of times – and never lived there.

We were without a meg – a penny – in our pockets or any real sense of the lingo to charm with. I'd sat in on a few Spanish classes back in St Gregory's, but French was a sexy-sounding mystery I was dying to get my tongue around.

Jamie could actually speak quite a bit of the language but refused to use it. I slipped into a big exaggeration, you know, the classic British habit of speaking English with a ridiculous French accent straight from 'Allo 'Allo. But I quickly picked up the lingo/swear words and expanded the vocabulary with a few basics.

'Eel a brolleir!' – translated means, 'Wanker'.
'Say Dagolas' – 'Filthy Dirty Rotten!'
'Merde!' – 'Shit'

We were staying in an apartment at the corner of Place Du Clichy, facing Clichy Cemetery. The lonely bone yard – a place of refuge where Jamie and I dossed down one night in the grave attendant's hut, a last resort if nowhere to stay, which occasionally happened.

But right now at the beginning of the Paris adventure we slept tight in each other's arms on a mattress in the living room of Peter Ogi, a Hungarian refugee and his girlfriend, Valerie. We met them en route and they knew Jamie's work.

The Cold War was still intense and the Iron Curtain in lock down at this time. Peter was one amazing fella – he told a funny story of his escape from Budapest by swimming the Blue Danube. He was a very gifted classically-trained concert pianist with a wicked sense of humour.

He dramatically drank 'Bull's Blood', the legendary Hungarian wine claiming it was the real thing when it's more like his home country's version of Guinness.

Peter was working on a forthcoming album and Jamie set to work straight away, designing and preparing the magical materials artwork for it. Peter idolised Jamie and was excited and delighted to have the master punk on his project.

As the friendship with the Hungarian couple developed, I found a new musician to work with in Peter and we co-created some songs around the piano, recording them on his 4-track studio at his home. A cracker of a little song flew out of the ether – titled Beauty and the Thief, a wistful lament to disco beats about a Bonnie and Clyde couple (the Paris tradition of love and romance were seeping in).

The demo for Beauty and the Thief became our calling card at numerous French record labels, whose doors opened eagerly to receive Jamie because of his Sex Pistols work and involvement with Malcolm McLaren and the making of Sid Vicious' My Way, which had been recorded for French Barclay records a couple of years before. Looking back we must have appeared so exotic to them, still under the influence of French crooning star Johnny Hallyday (a sort of Cliff Richard type).

Most of the companies were gobsmacked by the Svengali Punk and the flame-haired muse with the whitest face they'd ever seen, and signed us up with a cash advance that we buggered off with...we took the money and ran with the talent. We were certainly different from modern French singers as I daringly sang in French while their countrymen warbled in English.

There was lots of time to go sightseeing and one sunny afternoon we climbed the endless steps that lead to the Basilica of the Sacré-Coeur at Montmartre, which is built at the top of a high ridge where the bones of the 'Communards' of the French Revolution were buried.

Jamie knew some amazing stories of that stupendous uprising of the poor in Paris in 1745. Drinking in the history lesson, I asked him why so many aristocrats were rounded up and killed? Why didn't they run away? He said they were a 'peacock society' where the flamboyant rich were always on display – so easily spotted.

His words rang true, as I noticed while walking the boulevards how French people – men and women – would stop and gaze in admiration at their own reflection in conveniently-placed street mirrors totally without embarrassment. They peered and preened unselfconsciously. When I first walked the Paris streets I only had the nerve to check my reflection on the sly in the reflective image of parked cars, but as time went by I soon went native.

While looking down from Montmartre to the ancient city of Paris that stretched out to the River Seine and across the left bank, I became aware I was looking at a completely white dazzling city – shimmering Casablanca white with not a blade of green grass in sight. I asked Jamie: "Where's all the green grass gone?"

He laughed and told me: "We've left all the grass back home, Marg."

Nostalgia comes in colours as I missed the fecund greenery of Liverpool, but not the colour red as later that night I was swamped with it. It was May 1981, and a tribe of Liverpool FC supporters were amassed in the French capital for the European Cup final – against Real Madrid. The merry band of 'Reds Camp' followers had lost their way. They didn't have a clue, staggering around in the tiny street below.

I'd been drawn to the window when I heard our unmissable Liverpool twang filling the night air, arguing in confusion.

"Snazzer lad, it's deffo this one!"

They took off banging on the door of an old flop house up the street – to no luck. So I shouted down to them.

"Now then soft arse, the hotel's up here!"

About 30 dozen of them piled into the room and partied – I think Jamie was the only Fulham FC supporter there...

We returned from Paris for good in 1982 and took up residence in London, in a notorious squat called the barrier block in an austere, 70s tower block that lay on its side like a bull ring with tiny, slit windows.

A grey and foreboding building, it stood on Harbour Lane, Brixton.

It was hand-to-mouth time once again but, like back home in the north, we gravitated to the 'like minds' and chummed up with a motley crew from all over the country and beyond.

Jamie loved to show me his old haunts around London as he pointed out on the bus trundling along. He took me to South London and the Old Kent Road and his mother's family home – a 1920s semi with wonder gardens that joined the duck pond at the back.

Jamie would regale me with 'daring do' stories of rebel students at Croydon Art School with Malcolm McLaren and songwriter Robin Scott back in 1969. They staged a sit-in, a gesture of solidarity with the Paris uprising of 1968.

What a unique education I had from his first-class brain when on top of buses, or his guiding arm around me walking around the National Galleries. Jamie expanded my mind and broadened my awareness like nobody before.

His Druidic Scottish background excited and informed my life and art and his loyal support of the underdog chimed with mine.

Our on-going project from the beginning was called 'Leaving the Twentieth Century'.

A book Jamie had brought to my attention included many of his agi-pop illustrations put together by the leading 'Situationist' – Guy Debor – a French intellectual. I just loved to receive the flow of esoteric knowledge and spot-on observations that he poured into me.

With Jamie leading me on a guided tour of London, my generous teacher took me down Tin Pan Alley to survey where he and Malcolm McLaren once had an office called Glitter Best, conducting the Sex Pistols' affairs and then to the Cambridge Circus pub where we would sit in this busy West End bar for hours on end nursing a pint and plotting and planning our way to Gay Paree and a coming reunion and musical collaboration with Peter Ogi.

Jamie and I were busy falling in love and taking in some of the amazing Soho haunts. He took me to the Colony Rooms and the French House in Dean Street – old hands knew it as 'Frenchies.' It was a great, happening place to go if you didn't have the price of a pint, as there was always a boozed-up table full of champagne that over-flowed our way. The characters that frequented our way in Soho in the early 80s were still steeped in the traditions of British eccentricity and hugged the bars of Dean Street.

Robbie Coltrane – before he made it big – was great company and suited the Soho backdrop with his 1950s quiff and ready Scottish wit.

It would be years later when I met him again on the set of The Fruit Machine, written by our Frank. (He looked so comfortable and at ease in his big girls' frock). He played Annabelle, a transvestite character in the film shot in Liverpool and Brighton.

London was a great place to be in the 80s. Half of Liverpool was down there building for them – from Canary Wharf to Tower Bridge – all re-built by strong Scouse muscle. I still went back to Liverpool on a regular basis.

When I was hopping up and down from north to south I would race to catch the last train from Lime Street on a Sunday night – about 8pm. I would find it chocker with young Merseysiders coming from all directions carrying their kit bags. They filled the carriages to capacity and sang rock anthems all the way down to the Smoke. But they brought the dough home on Friday nights to their waiting families at home. I used to laugh at the irony of the idea put about that all Scousers are lazy.

At the time, we were staying at Westbourne Park and Portobello Road. Those places bring back sweet memories. I also lived in what could only be described as a 'mental' tower block called Chantry Point, otherwise known to us all as Sanitary Point. It was at the funky end of Elgin Avenue and not till years later did we find out it was riddled with asbestos. But, back then, it was a Godsend of a place – small but uniquely decorated with Jamie's paintings. It looked like a mini-version of the

Louvre. Just for a laugh, I taped off the living room like it was a living exhibition.

Boy George was a good friend of Jamie's in those days and he introduced me to him at the back of the charismatic fashion designer Vivienne Westwood's shop – The World's End on the King's Road. It was just before Boy George's big hit Karma Chameleon, which gave Culture Club their second UK number one and ended up topping the charts across the world after its release in 1983.

He was so strong, tall and handsome even though he was wearing his hair in ringlets – wearing more make-up than me – yet he still exuded full 'Man On' attitude and gabbed ten to the dozen and asked me, at one point, if I knew Pete Burns?

I calmed the waters as I knew they were rivals even then, as word went around Liverpool that *the* Pete Burns was metaphorically 'gunning' for Boy George as Pete had got there first with 'the look', and accused Boy George of ripping him off.

They were sort of fishing from the same river that flowed north to south.

It fascinated me that George and I could be distant cousins, because my grandmother's name on me mam's side is O'Dowd, just like the character I played in Blonde Fist – Ronnie O'Dowd. That was in homage to me mam's side of the family.

At one point in Chantry Point the next-door neighbour asked if he could have a bath in ours as his boiler had broken down. We hardly knew the fella but agreed to do him a turn and ran a nice soapy bath for him. He was a 'Crusty' who was busy helping demonstrations against the Tewksbury Bypass.

Once spruced up and dried out, he shared a cuppa and told us he was moving out of the next door flat across the landing the next morning. 'Hmmmm', I thought. I seized the opportunity to ask him if we could have the keys to the empty flat. He happily handed them over and our Frank moved in the very next day.

One night we had a dinner party in mine, attended by Malcolm McLaren and designer Judie Blaine – a brilliant influential stylist – who on many occasions dolled me up for the press.

The pair of them looked on bemused as a tray of roast potatoes came out of the oven, only to be whisked off by Frank across the landing to his place. The telephone wire also piped across the landing to Frank on the party line.

'That party was the party
to end all parties.
People were playing Beatles songs
all night long. Peter Firth and Alfred
Molina were there.
We had a couple of Russian
ambassadors
there too'

7. Brezhnev & Me

Me and our Frank have always been really, really close – he's only 12 months younger than me.

I ran off to Paris to try and become a singer and a star, and while I was there our Frank said: "Look, your name is Margi Clarke...NOT Petula Clarke, now...get home!"

He wrote Letter to Brezhnev while I was away, trying to find stardom somewhere else in another country. As it turned out, it was just like Dorothy in The Wizard of Oz because it was in my own back yard.

It was 1983 and we were all on the dole, but our Frank had written it, and he wanted to make it in Liverpool. We were living in a squat in a block of flats.

Nobody had any money. The shops donated our costumes and Lewis's the department store in town – now closed – gave us loads of stuff, including the famous red dress. You never saw a film set in those days in Liverpool, so people were so excited that they wanted to help.

You can see in the film that we were so skinny at the start. We didn't have any food, but my mum did the catering, and she fed us all up.

It was a happy set, which I think distils onto the screen.

But they were tough times. The miners' strike was on and Thatcher was battering the working classes. Liverpool in those days was so much quieter. Anyone who wanted to do anything creative went to London, so you couldn't get a Liverpool crew. The actors we used were all Scouse, but there just weren't camera operators or sound crews.

I remember when you walked down Seel Street you walked with the ghosts. Whole sections of the city were deserted because nobody wanted to invest. That film felt like a re-birth, something that helped to kick off the boom.

In those days the city's ship wasn't in. "When the cranes come down and we get the skyline back we'll have big films made here," we used to say. Now you walk down the streets and it feels like everything's happening.

I wouldn't say I had exactly the same personality as Teresa – my character in Letter to Brezhnev. I certainly haven't slept with as many men as she did. She's an archetypal Liverpool character, you know.

You get lots of girls – well I was one of them – who would all go out together of a night, and you didn't need money to have a good time in those days. You could go out with 50p and come back with the same 50p in your knickers.

Teresa was a classic Liverpool type, and what I like about that character is that she's all front. Alexandra Pigg's character is the winsome girl-next-door, and even though you'd think my character is the one who's got the guts – she hasn't.

She's like the lion in The Wizard of Oz again, she hasn't got the courage – it's Alexandra Pigg's character that has – and I think that's interesting.

I suppose as well, as an actress you do draw on some part of yourself when you're bringing the character to life.

There's an expression I use in one scene when I go over to the two Russian sailors in the club. I say: "I'll just go over and get a light off them", and I know in my head I'm thinking about filth – about sex. And I pull this expression, and I look the image of my mother. It freaked me out because I thought that's what my mother must be thinking when she looks like that.

Our Frank found the actress that ended up playing the mother in the film, Mandy Walsh – and she was so like our own mam. It's a great matriarchal character, based on all those amazing women who were shipped out from the city – they didn't leave Merseyside because then we'd all be away from the action – but they went to Kirkby. It's a place that gets so many shouts in the film, you know, it puts it on the map completely.

One of the great things about the film is that it's so brilliantly written. Every line of dialogue in it is carrying some gorgeousness to it. There were so many great lines I had in the film that really struck a chord with people.

You can always tell if a film's been well made from the attention paid to each little part, and in Brezhnev every little part is well written. And you know, if when you're making the film everyone gets on, well it goes on to the celluloid – it's distilled into the movie.

The initial budget for Letter to Brezhnev was £50,000 – that would be the cocaine budget on a Rambo movie, that's what our Frank jokingly said. It was released at the same time as My Beautiful Launderette, which was made for about two million but was still cited as a low budget film. But four times as many people went to see Brezhnev than went to see My Beautiful Launderette.

Another thing to remember about the time when Brezhnev was written – Russia was considered to be the evil empire. So to make that film then, when Thatcherism was just getting going and becoming more and more powerful – that was a really brave and strong thing to do.

The film wasn't lost on the Thatcher government either, you know. They watched it, you bet they did.

The scene in the taxi, with the wonderful Carl Chase as the taxi driver, well, there's a line when Alexandra says to me: "I thought you weren't going to pay him?" and I reply: "Yeah, but he's one of us."

They soon picked that line up. Everyone quoted lines from the film to me, especially within the gay community – and that was instrumental in helping to promote it.

Alexandra Pigg was baby sitter to our Laurence and was a budding actress, with girl-next-door, winsome looks. She was like a buxom version of the Darling Buds of May character played by Catherine Zeta Jones. A real man eater, with the best jugs in the business.

I pleaded with our Frank to play the part of Elaine – the romantic lead – but he said no. He wanted me to wear a "twat hat" and be the chicken stuffer Teresa, who's stuffing arm could pack 200 birds in a shift.

I think Frank was right, his casting eye worked perfectly with Alexandra. We were more like sisters and fell so easily into the work together.

I still keep in touch with Alexandra through Facebook, but I haven't seen her for years. She got married and went to live in the States, but has since moved back.

She's a writer now. She once rang me up from LA when she was having a dinner party. I asked her what she was making and she said it was Almond Soup! I asked: "What is wrong with a pan of Scouse?"

And, of course, one of the unsung heroes of the film is Bruce McGowan, who sadly passed away a few years ago.

He shot the movie, and I remember we had a screening at the Philharmonic Hall. He'd already been given a terrible diagnosis and was not well at all, but he legged it like a young man into the hall to see the film for one last time. And he really is an unsung hero, because if you look at the film you will see how beautifully it was captured.

Little shots, like the one of Eberle Street. That's the scene were Peter and Elaine stop to look at the moon shining above the rooftops, the same silvery moon shining in Russia as it did, and does, in Liverpool.

How long have we had that street? It goes back to city charter times of 1207, and it's still with us. How lovely it looked. The whole town looked beautiful. The State nightclub on Dale Street was also central to the early scenes in the film. That's where we met the sailors on the night out. That was such an iconic club in the 80s. It really took off after the film's success.

When we made the film Liverpool didn't have a tourist board that would cash in on things like films, and we certainly didn't have a Film Office or anything like it. We all knew the Pier Head, but we'd never seen the top of the Liver Building.

It wasn't until we saw Letter to Brezhnev that we saw that the Liver Bird had eggs. So the film showed us aspects of the city that we'd never set eyes on.

And Brezhnev also captured aspects of our city's character – there's a natural aggressiveness. Liverpool is a Scorpio city – that was the ascendant sign when the charter was signed. That aggression was perfectly shown in the chip shop scene, when the Liverpudlian argues with Igor and keeps trying to head butt...and misses.

It's aggressive, but funny at the same time. I often think if aliens were observing us from a space ship they'd think we were always about to batter one another. That scene captures that perfectly.

We were really lucky with all our actors as well. Peter Firth got involved because we knew his wife – Peter had just finished working on a 25 million dollar movie, and when Frank said he'd agreed to play a lead in Brezhnev, he thought we were just running around Liverpool with some super eight – 8mm film.

He played the part of Peter, and he had no idea it was going to be so well executed and that it would turn out to be such a massive hit. But good on him, because he could have come over all high status and said no.

The same goes for Fred Molina (Alfred). Alfred was a great kisser and wonderful to work with. He is one of those instinctive actors who is still going strong today. They give a certain gravitas, or weight to it. And you know, people thought they were REAL Russians when we were filming in town.

Mind you, when the camera pulled away from the Kremlin shot, you'd have sworn it was Russia, and it was Birkenhead!

Neil Cunningham – who played the Foreign Office man – sadly we've lost him as well. He died like a lot of our friends in those times of an AIDS-related illness...but he was an inspiring actor with a lovely posh voice who loved working on the film – he couldn't get enough of us. So there were a lot of people who put their faith in the film, and what a success it was.

There were two fabulous parties I remember after Brezhnev. The premiere night was up in Kirkby despite Palace Pictures trying to strong arm our Frank into agreeing to wine and cheese in London.

He said: "No way. I'm not having it. The premiere has got to be in Kirkby." They said that none of the stars would go there.

Frank just said: "We don't care. We're the stars anyway. It's got to be shorts and pints mate or no one's going!"

So it was our Frank sticking to his colours that produced that fantastic party. People still talk about it because over three thousand people turned up, including cast, crew, stars, celebrities and the people of Kirkby.

People were fighting for tickets for it. It was all free. It was videoed, and what used to always make my dad laugh was when we used to play the tape he would always say: "Look at all the ale they've got on that table!" The premiere had that feel of something from the 1920s. It looked like Dynasty – Joan Bakewell came up to Kirkby to our house, and I was so proud of my sisters – they looked drop dead gorgeous.

People were bunking in through the toilet windows. I let them in because I felt terrible that there were Kirkby people locked outside. To get an invite, you had to be involved in it. It was the first time in Liverpool that anyone had done a premiere like that, at source, where the idea came from.

At the party afterwards we had at least three hundred people in my mother's council house, at about one o'clock in the morning. There were loads of people in the garden in Northwood. Mum's family were well known locally in Everton for throwing great parties in the twenties. They were the original 'roll out the barrel' gang.

I don't know why there's no photographs of that occasion. I've never taken photographs. If you came into my house there's not one picture of me. I'm not interested. I don't even carry them. I travel very light. I've got a great memory.

That party was the party to end all parties. We won at all levels. It went on right through until the next day. People were playing Beatles songs all night long. Peter Firth and Alfred Molina were there. We had a couple of Russian Ambassadors there too.

They gave us two awards – mine was made out of bottle tops and Sandra's was made out of cigarette packets. They were our Oscars off the Russians. I loved it because they were so down to earth. I don't know what's happened to that award – it's around somewhere.

The other 'do' we had was when we were nominated for the Evening Standard British Film Awards, which was held at the Savoy. It's as beautiful as the Adelphi. I'll never forget that experience.

Our limo from Euston Station pulling up, the Clarke Clan arriving and were booked – courtesy of the film's distributors into a pretty suite of rooms.

Me, Jamie my mum and dad, Frank and Angela.

We unpacked our bags, opened the fridge full of drinks – we got stuck in and made excited preparations for that night's awards.

In the entry for 'Best Newcomer' Alexander Pigg and I had a good chance. Our Angela, who was only about 16, revelled in the excitement and attention plied by the make-up artist, combing her long wavy hair around huge rollers.

She had hardly left Kirkby before and loved 'getting it on'.

I was nowhere near ready.

I still had to find a dress to wear. I needed something extra special and new. I had decided against packing the 'high tech'-looking peach Yamamoto suit, coupled with silver space-age shoes.

It was the outfit I'd worn six months before for the premiere of Brezhnev in Kirkby. As a last resort, I brought with me the famous 'red dress' – the one I wore as the character Teresa in the film, just in case – against the odds – I couldn't find anything to wear.

The odds shortened as I paced up and down the King's Road, coming in and out of boutiques empty-handed.

Back at the hotel, Frank said: "You're not giving up – go and find something glam and powerful. But not the red dress – that was Teresa.

"You are NOT Teresa."

I jumped a cab to Soho, needless to say.

I went to a famous shop, Patisserie Valerie in Old Compton Street, and I was slumped in a chair. It was 3pm.

Then two gay rescuers walked in – devotees of the film.

They were really excited to see me and I poured out my story like Cinderella. I couldn't go to the ball – just four hours away.

We all went to world-famous designer Anthony Pierce's place in Covent Garden and there it was – this black floor-length gown with designer 'buffer' across the chest, reflecting the elegance of the sirens of the '20s.

I looked like I was going down on the Titanic.

So it took two fab fairies to make this girl ready for the party.

Back at the Savoy...

I made an acceptance speech, along with Alexandra after we had been announced, jointly, as 'Best Newcomer'. I was guttural next to the tinkling glasses going on at the tables.

UNTIL...

George Harrison went on stage and said: "Hello", in that warm Scouse accent. He quite rightly won an award for HandMade Films.

After the awards, I made it my business. I just had to go and speak to him.

I did, and I said: "George, I only wanted to be famous so I could shag John Lennon – but he's popped off."

George looked at me and smiled: "Well, Margi, I'm a Beatle too, you know."

After the ceremony there was another Clarke party in our suites, with Daniel Day-Lewis, Twiggy and David Puttnam there.

My mam Frances was there, and my dad Mick (uncomfortable in his penguin suit) was stripped down to his vest.

He picked up the silver room service tray and silver spoon (the first time he had ever had one – and the last) and did the Sheik of Arabic.

It was like Rab C. Nesbitt.

Daniel Day-Lewis, who's shy anyway, didn't want to do a turn. He didn't say much – his eyes spoke volumes.

But David Puttnam did, and burst into a squeaky version of the classic song There's No Business Like Show Business.

My mam told him to sit down

"Don't call us – we'll call you."

The end of another perfect day.

Room service sent up bottle after bottle of pure crystal vodka.

We toasted Brezhnev. We toasted each other.

We also went to Cannes for the festival, in 1985, and I was sitting next to Mel Gibson watching our film. He fascinated me, because he reminded me of someone from Scotland Road – he had a cow's lick. The film got me and Alex carried out the cinema (we weren't legless just then). It was an amazing never-to-forget moment.

I think a part of the success of the film came from the response to the message the film sent out. People didn't really want to have all this aggression towards other human beings in Russia, and Brezhnev was the first to publicly show that. It did something really important because it softened the hardness of the western world's attitude. It put a stop to all those gung-ho, moronic Rambo-style movies where they were murdering Russians all the time.

As for Teresa, I often wondered what happened to her. When the movie ended she was still in Russia. Whether she stayed there or not, who knows? We'll never know – but what I'm certain of is that all our lives moved on from that point. Nothing was the same after that.

'I am a very good
friend of Dorothy's.
And I'll never stop
looking for the Wizard.
I'm stlll looking over the
rainbow —
aren't we all?'

8. A Friend of Dorothy's

Getting the money together for Brezhnev was almost like a film in itself. Someone should make a movie of how Frank put it together.

I was delighted when the Castelton family backed the film, because I'd read an article in The Guardian on them, and how they had given away shares in the company to their workers.

They were venture capitalists with a small 'c'. They had foresight because they were listening to the same brand of propaganda that we were, and yet they had the guts to back it.

It was through Frank's chance meeting with Fiona Castelton that Brezhnev got started. He was invited to their house in the Isle of Man and they became interested in putting up funds for the film. They saw that it was a powerful story.

It was a groundbreaking film – it was the first movie to have a pop music score – although that had an adverse effect on me in a sense, because I did some of the music in Brezhnev with Alan Gill, the legendary guitarist from The Teardrop Explodes.

My dad had always drummed this into me – you train your ego like you train your bowel and your bowel's full of shit.

I could deal with the press because I'd been trained up at Granada when I was Margox, and that was what gave me the initial confidence to be able to go out and know, on camera, what was the most important thing to bring to attention.

The overriding theme of the film was Love and Peace, and that was why we won an award off the Catholic Humanities Society.

My mother was made up, and the Bishop came to Cannes to give us the award. I asked him how come he had given us this award, and he turned around and said it was because it was about love and peace.

That was when I felt I was a star. I'd wanted to become one since I was seven, and now I really felt like I was a star.

It turned my head with myself, not how I behaved to other people. They were the wonder years. Everything was peaked with extra energy. I had money in my pocket. The wonder years lasted until my mother passed away, when I started to go into the wilderness years.

But Brezhnev was definitely the start of the good period.

Of course I've got an ego, but it goes from the sublime to the ridiculous. I can be outrageously egotistical one minute, and dead humble the next. I was a good laugh then.

I still had all my mates up in Liverpool, but Jamie and I had moved from Hartington Road in Liverpool and were living in London then. I think I have got less of a showbiz ego now. That drive for attention – I had to face up to that, and I can take it or leave it.

With Brezhnev I felt like I'd won the race – and I've always been fast on my feet.

I've legged it all the way through my own life. I've always given it toes. I was glorying in lifting the trophy up in the air. That's ego.

Later on, the footballer Stan Collymore told me a story about ego – about the gladiators and how they were huge stars; how when they won a tournament they went on a tour of the streets in a chariot, and how all the people lined the streets to see them. And inside the chariot was a little dwarf, and when the people were shouting telling them they were gods, the dwarf would say: "No you're not, you're nothing, take no notice of them."

So when my ego grew, I'd have to shrink it because I was still me – born in Sandhills, raised in Kirkby.

But the industry didn't quite know how to place me, in the aftermath of Brezhnev. I'd had that in Margox days as well – Granada didn't keep hold of me. They trained me up for 12 months and then let me go. It was such a big character that I'd played, with a strong tongue and they didn't know quite how I fitted in.

Me and Jamie were still working on our Leaving The Twentieth Century creative collaboration. That side of me as a very serious artist didn't want to sell out, didn't want to go mainstream. We wanted to deliver our stuff. So I did a version of that – it was all about taking our ideas into the 21st century.

And then I wasn't offered any work.

I don't know why – it was a mystery.

Alexandra went on to do something called Smart Money. She was a good actress and went down to London. As I've said I was also living there in Elgin Avenue, which led onto Westbourne Park. Our asbestos-riddled tower block Chancery Point was like the structure of the class system, because on the top were the people who had the right to be there because they had proper rent books, and we were squatting in the middle.

And this was in the days of Lady Tesco – Lady Porter – who was busy selling off cemeteries. Where we were was a Labour stronghold, and the Tories were gerrymandering, moving all the Labour people out and putting all the yuppies in.

So it was an interesting time, but like I say, I didn't get any work offers.

We didn't make loads of money from Brezhnev either. I made eight thousand pounds as an actress, and being from Kirkby at that time it sounded massive. And it was.

But I didn't go and audition for that role – we produced that ourselves – and I also thought that wasn't taken into account. I'd done the title song, too, which paid me £1000 – but I didn't have any protection from an agent to negotiate for me.

The second thing I did in England after that was Making Out, and I had to wait a long time for that.

Of course that knocked my confidence, I was back to having no money – that side has never really left me – but you learn how to get by, and you help each other out. At least, as we were squatting in London, we didn't have to worry about the rent.

I did get a load of attention from members of the public after Brezhnev, though – I was really privileged. People would come up to me and say fantastic things to me.

If they had said nasty things then I wouldn't have liked it. People felt like they knew me because they'd seen themselves in the movie. They'd jangled in the toilets about what fellas they fancied, just like me and Alexandra did in the film. They only had tuppence to go out with but they'd have a brilliant time.

I think they also recognised by what I was saying in interviews that I was flying our flag.

At that time, Liverpool was a dirty word. We were in the middle of Thatcherism and we were the last place in England that resisted. So that was quite a tough period. People knew that my colours were tied to the mast. And you had to walk your talk.

I did.

But I was in danger of becoming a 'one-hit wonder'. At least Frank marshalled himself and did The Fruit Machine, which had a big impact on the gay scene.

Despite that, I still loved how Brezhnev regenerated me, our family and Liverpool. That's one of the feelings that will always stay with me. Our family got to tell the time to the world. That's powerful. Every time I hear that music, it's like the national anthem, I don't know whether to stand up or sit down.

There were two scenes that I was never given that I think I should have got. One was where I go over to ask for a light – there should have been a little exchange there.

And I thought that the hotel scene should have been bigger.

But Brezhnev was totally of its time.

I think we got about 30 awards for it.

There was another consequence of Brezhnev. I became a gay icon, and it's something that has stayed with me ever since.

To be honest, if it hadn't have been for the gay community I would have starved, gone without, left to wither on the vine. But I was blessed with gay friends in show business and my closest mates at home have given me loving energy just when I needed it most.

Even at the beginning as Margox, with all the producers and directors to be found in television and acting worlds, it was my gay co-creatives that had the guts to employ me!

It seems like at times as if every door was closed to me – no room at the inn. And it was then my 'brothers and sisters', who gaily opened a work-giving window to reality TV and one-off appearances, keeping the wolf at bay.

Like electrical currents that picked me up when in the days after my mother passed away, I was prone to going right down to the bottom of the river.

My best friend, 'Lady Shaun' has the wonderful gift of happiness and has been at my side in tough times, lending me glam clothes for auditions that I never seemed to get.

Looking back now, I can understand why casting directors are paid huge amounts of money to be able to spot the actors who have addiction issues and, in the wilderness years, I did.

At least I still stood out in Shaun's wonderful clothes.

The fantastic designer gear I owned from the '80s and '90s have long gone after a life lived on castors.

Like most mums I dress in jeans and jumper – the practical look that goes well with being a lone parent on 'planet Mum.'

On the occasion of a big night out, Shaun 'it takes a fairy to make things pretty' will take great pleasure in 'dollin' up the doll' with sparkle and spangle – coming with my own lights he sends me out into the waiting world.

I love meeting and being around other people and during my millions of train rides up and down the country from north to south and back sometimes in the same day, I met some incredible up-lifting people full of life love and passion – like the young gay lad I met going to London on his very first date.

I picked up his heart's intent straight away and encouraged his leap into his awakening sexuality.

He – the young man I shared a carriage to the capital with – is now 20 years later the editor of a leading gay magazine.

Well, good for him.

Show business makes perfect sense. It's the safest and most fulfilling industry if you have a flamboyant personality and a campness that won't go in a box or be pigeon holed.

Let's face it, you are never going to be welcome on a building site or factory floor but can flourish and thrive when the showbiz curtain goes up.

I remain really grateful for the loving support of my gay 'family'.

We recognise each other everywhere we go; at work, on the streets and in cyber space.

A massive legion of friends walking through life together.

I can remember my mam bravely going on Doctor Miriam Stoppard's Granada TV show in the mid-1980s in a public defence of the gay community who, for them, in those far off Thatcher days were being demonised by the head of Manchester Police.

Police chief James Anderton, a professed Christian, I believe stoked up people's prejudice and intolerance with outrageous, offensive comments about 'our family and friends' dying of HIV.

My mother, a lifelong follower of Jesus Christ, had no problem accepting people's different sexuality and viewed it as a part of what it is to be human.

Like the natural leader she was, she stood up to be counted and assured Dr. Miriam that:

"Love can only be a good thing."

'Queenie in Making Out came
along at the right time. I was fed
up waiting for roles.
I was decorated like a frigging
shire horse with awards galore
– but no jobs.
I actually thought about just
going back to pulling men
or pints'

9. Making Out

It was when I was in London that I started the wheels in motion for an ambitious photographic project.

The long boardroom in the office building in Soho Square was the headquarters of the PR company Ogilvy and Mather, who were taking care of the contract – a photographic assignment for the television insider magazine Campaign.

Campaign was the leading trade magazine of the advertising world and where I was due for a meeting with producers at 2pm. I had often flicked through a copy in the many foyers and well-stocked reception lounges waiting to audition various roles. It was an up-to-the-minute read amazingly connected to the communications hive, and always worth a skim.

In this case, the advertisers' remit was to ask a group of celebrities about their television viewing habits (creative for me as I didn't then and still don't watch television), basically what they: a) viewed; b) liked; c) had an opinion on.

And, after approval, to photographically re-enact their favourite showbiz icons and scenarios.

I was dressed that early summer's afternoon of 1991 sexy but smart in a blue Margaret Howell well-tailored dress and Maud Frizon shoes.

I felt on top of the world.

Working it, bobbin' down Oxford Street weaving through the crowds of people purposely on my way to the meeting.

Imagining the coming encounter would they – the bosses – be open-minded to my interpretation and ideas?

Could they think outside the box? Or would I be rebuffed? Or, worse still, see my ideas used in some media...further down the line, which was sometimes the case.

But I needn't have worried about anyone being too square to handle what was coming as I was greeted enthusiastically in an elongated room full of bright, very young men who looked and dressed like 'Spiral Tribe' ravers still on an E.

I was happy and relieved it wasn't the stifling-stuffed suits, but this happy band of highly creative young bucks – many of them the best brains in advertising.

They eagerly leaned across the table closer as I got into my 'gem tale' pitch, as I called it, and proposed exactly where – and how – I wanted to have my picture taken.

"I want to be a 21st century bondage fairy at Stonehenge", I announced.

No problem to these lads, the only issue was at which part the stones were coming in!

Ironic when you think that the country was still in 'Thatcher mode' and nobody – not even the Druid Priest for Summer Solstice – were let anywhere near the stones.

It was only a few years before when the Tory government violently attacked the peace-loving hippies at what is now remembered as 'The Battle of the Beanfield', which went down in hippy folklore.

Well, these lads were their younger brothers and lapped it up. I got full approval from the ravin' pill poppin' advertisers!

I described, in some detail, the costume I would wear as the 21st century 'Bondage Fairy'. On the breast plate of the dress was a bold print of Boadicea in full battle cry and painted by Jamie.

The beautiful shimmering dress was made by the brilliant London designer Michael Nichols. He had come to prominence making and designing the rhinestone corset that Tammy Wynette wore in the 'far out there' single Justified & Ancient by KLF who, later with Blonde Fist, generously allowed us to use their single What Time is Love for the soundtrack of the film.

I also told them I would bring along for the shoot my incredible, radiant power-packed magic halogen wand that when I pressed, a concealed button buried in the stem lit up like a street lamp. It was stunning, and Stonehenge was calling me in quite at dark time to shine the light.

The young men all up for it introduced me to the photographer. A curly-hair introspective Frenchman called Pierre nervously shook my hand. I began to tell him the little bit of knowledge that Jamie the Druid had told me, and asked if I could bring Jamie along with me – only to be told that it was a closed shoot and only the essential people would be there. I tried to inform him how 'essential' Jamie – together with Stonehenge – were, but was met with a glazed expression.

I was well excited to be part of a privileged assignment to Britain's most ancient site, to be amongst the blue Sarson stones, the most sacred structure to the Druids and deeply ingrained in the nation's psyche

Advertising companies like the one I was now employed by had used Stonehenge extensively to convey their commercial message since advertising began.

Jamie told me that the Stones were like some astrological clock reflecting the times we live in and in 1991, and today, the site is run by British Heritage or 'British Heretics' as I like to call them.

Two days later we set out on the journey to Wiltshire on a luxury coach, ludicrously big for just me, the late Chris Diggle and Beverley Pond Jones – two good friends and brilliant appliers of make-up. They could turn base metal to gold. They did that for me on Blonde Fist.

The pair of them stretched out on the backseat surrounded by picnic goodies, beckoned me to get stuck into the buffet and join in the juicy gabs as we sped along the M4 motorway to Wiltshire.

About 10 miles into the journey, when I was having bright red lipstick applied by Bev, the tyre blew out with a bang and had us pulled over onto the hard shoulder. We were marooned, and had to wait for replacement transport to get us on our way. One hour later, another ludicrously large coach pulled up and the three of us jumped on board and once again took our seats at the back.

As the coach raced along a quiet stretch of the road, just as Chris was carefully rollin' a spliff and Beverley was teezin' the curls in my hair to stand up we had another blow out! The same front tyre made a similar dramatic explosion and we were off the coach again...

Sitting in the production car that picked us up like abandoned refugees from a yet-to-happen rave was our friend, the French photographer Pierre.

I sidled next to him and told him straight: "If you'd have invited the Druid none of this coach karma would have happened!"

Once we got there I was humbled, in awe at the sheer intelligent wonder of Stonehenge and immediately felt its masculine energies. They moved me with courage to sing out at the top of my voice – all of the struggling causes of humanity...

'Universal Majesty,
Love Infinite
End The War
Feed The People'

Well, you know what I mean. A few years later, another photographic assignment would get me noticed for an entirely different reason. I posed nude while nine months' pregnant with my daughter Rowan. It was a take on the famous Vanity Fair spread with Demi Moore and was published to much acclaim.

It was also while I was in London that I was offered the part of Queenie in Making Out. Queenie was the ringleader at an electronics factory – a series about love, hates and humiliations of six women workers.

During Making Out, a journalist from the Press Association interviewed me and said I was the 'Marilyn Monroe of Merseyside.' He also said because of our talented family that we were 'The Von Traps of Kirkby.' I told him: "Look, I am just a Kirkby girl through and through." What would my family and friends think if I started talking all posh and playing the big star?" I told him straight I'd never be able to get off at Lime Street station ever again if I started acting like that. I always gave good copy – still do.

It was great back in the late '80s and early '90s doing Making Out with such a fantastic crew. I was 36 when I made that and now 20 years on, I'm still one of the girls and treated like one of the girls, which is how it should be.

I don't get fame attacks. You are what you are. I am what I am.

At the time, I was still with Jamie and he proposed every Tuesday night for seven years.

I used to say to him: "Let's sort it out on Friday..."

But Friday was always Bingo night so we never got round to it.

I recall telling the press at the numerous media get-togethers we had that Queenie – the character – would never calm down. Queenie used to tell her on-screen hubby 'Chunky': 'Start talking respectability and I'll show you a polished pair of hooves.' I love that line.

My Queenie was such a new lease of life – she came at the right time because I was fed up waiting for acting roles. I was actually, at the time, thinking of going out to pull pints to make a living.

Then along came factory femme fatale Queenie. There was probably a bit of me in Queenie's character – I discovered Revlon at the age of 11.

In my own past there were times when I would have happily gone out with no knickers on than have no mascara.

Making Out was my first major TV work following Brezhnev and came not before time and to my rescue   a relief coming as it did after an 18-month work hiatus.

In my naivety I thought that after all the awards I'd won, decorated like a frigging shire horse, that I would be inundated with TV offers. After all, this pet could win prizes. I couldn't wait to act again on set, preparing for this factory girl called Queenie.

I didn't like the name at first. I told producer John Chapman: "You don't get called Queenie until you're 50, and the only thing I'm not pushing is a pram".

My sisters Eileen and Mo had both worked in factories so naturally tuned me into the working rhythm. I can say hand on my heart I had the time of my life on writer Debbie Horsfield's brilliant drama, and for three ratings-winning series at prime time on BBC1.

Queenie was a great character – brash, tough, outrageous but with a heart of gold. But you know I was not like Queenie. No, no, no.

We only looked alike. I am real, she was a fantasy. I was just acting a part but while recording it the things she said – her attitude – reminded me more of when I was seven. I'll probably be like her when I'm 70.

Making Out was one of those rare shows where the women were allowed to get the better of the blokes. Instead of the usual stereotypes – fluttering females – the women were blunt and bawdy. I was proud to be depicting a real woman. A strong matriarchal character who stood up for the girls – her co-workers at the electronics factory.

The series was set in a historic old chimney-stacked cotton mill – an incredible backdrop to playing the Lancashire town of Duckenfield. It had brilliant scripts and an outstanding cast of accomplished players, including Rachel Davies.

Rachel, so professional, helped me keep my head together during the tough schedule. She is dead funny and a generous artist who taught me a lot about acting. Moya Brady, who played the cracking character Klepto, brought on set loads of youthful enthusiasm. Moya came with me once in my pink Ford Cortina (Walnut Dash Mark 2) all the way to the Johnny Todd pub in Kirkby to meet local hero Terry Hickey.

Red-haired Heather Tobias, another well-accomplished actress, gave us girls tango lessons as we waited, bored between set-ups. It was such a strong female cast. It was unusual then – and even now – to have a production with so many good parts for women. It was a stroke of genius from Debbie. She captured the time so well when men, like my TV hubby Chunky, were out of work.

Tracie Bennett had come to rightful acclaim in Corrie years before I got there. She'd already played every theatre in the West End and is a strong, versatile performer. I loved her natural Northern approach and giant raucous laugh – she's only tiny, but she played the kitten that roars.

Oh and there was our Shirley. Shirley Stelfox. She gave me a really useful tip when trying to keep my eyes from going cross-eyed (which mine did if I tried too hard).

And then there was Keith Allen. He played Sexy Rexy, the factory boss. I'll always remember one day when we were playing an all-cast scene that went on forever to record. Keith thought he'd pump things up a little – he let off a bottle of party poppers on set. Us girls went bright red in the gob and looked like we were practicing for a heart attack – for real. We all used to say to Keith you are the UK's Jack Nicholson   he loved that. It was his soft spot.

We had such a laugh on that show, equipped as we were with a young rule-breaking maverick like Keith who joined forces with a 'well up for it' Gary Beadle, who on set copped a load of stick as the factory gopher (go for this...go for that).

Keith and Gary would later cause double trouble at the Britannia Hotel, where the cast stayed. We counted 16 British Caledonian air hostesses going in and out of Keith's room in a week.

They kept us well behaved actresses – in comparison – on our toes and highly entertained.

Even my dad got a kick out of it. He enjoyed giving me the occasional lift to work singing George Formby songs such as 'That Miser Was Wiser', all the way up the East Lancs Road.

Just before he opened the car door to let me out at the factory gate, he loved to say: "Well, Margi, I never thought I'd see a girl of mine working in the mills."

Making Out was the longest and happiest production I was ever involved in. Those times are now long gone; crazy days and a summer of love in Manchester.

We really felt then: "Is the North on the rise again?" Even the music for the series by Manc band New Order was ground-breaking. We were on a winner and the public loved it. We equally loved working on it – and it showed.

Melanie Kilburn's contribution to Making Out was crucial as she gave a superb performance as Jill, the harrassed housewife who reluctantly goes out to work.

When I first met Melanie in rehearsals I think my upfront, 'tell it like it is' approach left her stunned and we started out wary of each other. But by the end of the first series, we became good friends. It was Melanie who taught me how to throw away a line of dialogue by not putting any emotion in it.

My on-screen husband was played by actor and former member of the Flying Pickets a cappella band Brian Hibbard (they had a number one hit with Only You in 1983). He would arrive at work delighted – with a big smile on his face. I would call out to him as he came into make-up.

"Good morning Brian lad, how are yer?"

He always answered the same way and said he was doing: "Bastard marvellous."

Now, 20 years later, I am still asked why the popular series has never been repeated and to this day I can only guess that it's political.

Who knows, one day I might be a Duckie girl again, back with all the girls in the mill.

I recently looked back at an old copy I had of the Radio Times in 1989. As I flicked back through the pages, I had a look at what was on the TV schedules.

It felt like a lot of the programmes were either set in a mansion house or were either stuck in a time warp – historical dramas and all the rest of it. Making Out stood out then – because it was the only drama about real people.

I'm proud of my role in it and the fact that it went on for so long goes to show how big a success it was.

'Blonde Fist was originally called
Raging Cow.
I played Ronnie O'Dowd,

the K.O. queen.

That film is ultimately about
life and death'

10. Follow that Blonde

I could have 'sold out' after Brezhnev and made millions from doing certain films, but I didn't. Blonde Fist came into being because I went and did a film in Berlin.

It was called Helsinki Naples All Night Long – I was playing a prostitute – with one of the Kaurismaki brothers, Mika Kaurismaki, the renowned Finnish film director.

It was when I was beginning to travel abroad. I was really excited to have the opportunity to go to places I'd never have been able to go to before. It stimulated me. I was really intrigued by how different everything was from Liverpool. And when I got to Berlin, they sent a limousine to pick me up

This was two years after Letter to Brezhnev. I hadn't had any major roles and it looked like all that had been for nothing. But then who called me to work with them? These European directors.

So I hopped into the limo, all made up with myself. The driver's taking me, and at this time the Berlin Wall was still up. I'd had the idea that the wall went straight across from the East to the West, so it completely shocked me when I found out that the Wall was completely circular and surrounded the West. I was looking out of the window and I kept saying to the driver: "Oh, that's a lovely building, that, lad", and he'd reply: "Yah, that's und East."

Everything that I liked was in the East. It was amazing because the western part of Berlin, architecturally, was like this big Capitalistic tease. It had every type of architecture you could think of and the biggest neon lights, and the biggest BMW sign – all flashing at Eastern Berlin.

The Western architecture didn't interest me. What was in the East was beautiful – all old, romantic, odd architecture. I asked: "Wasn't the East bombed during the war?"

And the driver said yes they were. But what they did, apparently, in the West, they put all the rubble from the bombed buildings and put it in a park, whereas in the East they used the rubble to rebuild what had been bombed.

So there I am in Berlin on my way to play the last prostitute in Berlin, at the request of the Kaurismaki brothers.

I'd asked Aki Kaurismaki what his name meant and he said it was the name of a dog, in Finnish. The brothers were like our Frank and me. They'd both plotted and planned, from childhood, to deliver this dream in film. When the two of them were working as kitchen orderlies in a hotel in Gothenburg, they had been to see Letter to Brezhnev and they both absolutely loved it, and thought it was really funny.

Aki turned to Mika and said: "Follow that Blonde."

Where they were really clever, was that not only did they make their own films, but they also bought their own cinema. So then they had a distribution outlet, and that's how they built their film base. So they called me over to work with them in Berlin, and I got a contract to work with Aki.

I was there, and I loved going wandering off on my own, and I'm walking around and there was this big poster of Rambo, which had followed on from Rocky. Now Rambo couldn't have been more diametrically opposed to what we were doing.

Letter to Brezhnev sort of knocked Rambo off its perch. It wasn't so much that it was the underdog, it was more about what did the underdog do when it became top dog? He went and murdered loads of Russians.

Well, we put a stop to that with Brezhnev, that was all over.

So I'm standing looking at this poster, and there's Rambo with a big machine gun, and the headline was: *'Crime is the Illness. This is the Cure.'* It made me laugh. The cure was in the sickness.

I suddenly thought, 'what if this Rambo/Rocky character was a woman?' That's how Blonde Fist first came to me. I got lots of ideas but not many of them would go into production. I got on to our Frank and said I'd love to play a boxer. The light went on immediately with Frank, because he knew only too well how many battles I'd fought on his behalf as a kid. It was best for me to keep the ideas within the clan. I'd tried to go outside the family and put myself up for work, and I was left waiting. So it made every sense to do it with our Frank.

After Brezhnev, he had done The Fruit Machine. There wasn't a role for me in that but it was a brilliant story because it was cathartic for Frank and he brought 'his' story to it.

And then two years later he was going to write me a new vehicle.

So Blonde Fist was inspired by Rocky in a sort of role reversal way. You have a strong archetype, and then you reverse it – make it female. And then you've got a whole different perspective, which appeals to 50 per cent of your audience. The other 50 per cent will be interested if you're going to get it right. That was one of the things that I aimed to do with Blonde Fist.

I had to get that right. I hadn't seen Rocky, I wasn't that movie literate to be honest but I devoured newsprint. Yet this poster, with the Rambo/Rocky persona, made me laugh. That gun triggered something in me, and I started to think about me playing a female gladiator – a super strong woman. It reminded me of great stories that Jamie had taught me, about Boadicea, Queen Mab, and the Welsh Queen Guinevere. Jamie Reid was my university, and he gave me historical understanding of these fantastic female characters.

So all those Celtic tales of women warriors resonated with back home in Liverpool, with women running the home – as in other working-class cities – a matriarchal society. All that led up to Blonde Fist.

When I rang Frank with the concept of Blonde Fist, he loved the idea – it stimulated him and inspired him, and he started writing it. I didn't write one word of it – I had no more ideas after that initial one – but Frank came up with the title Raging Cow.

When I was filming on Helsinki Naples, there were two old-time stars in it. One was Sam Fuller, who is widely credited as a leading light in 'Film Noir'. He used to be a reporter on the Chicago Tribune and I think he was the first journalist to ride what's called 'cop car bucket seat' with the police – going to raids.

He did all of the underworld crime stories, and was left of field. Sam was really quite radical – he'd done a cracking little film called Cracked Corridor, about a journalist who goes into a sanatorium just to follow a story. Of course he had to pretend he was mad, and in the end he becomes mad. He made another film about racism called White Dog. Aki Kaurismaki absolutely worshipped him.

Sam was in his eighties at this time, smoked a big cigar and he reminded me of an archetypal Noir figure like Eliot Ness. He had a lovely big German wife who protected him from everyone.

The other old-time actor knew someone who was married to Joan Crawford. It so happened that Sam also used to go out with her and he used to tell me all about his former life with Ms Crawford.

I used to sit and gab with him in between scenes and he used to tell me all about how good Joan was in bed, and then he told me how he got kicked out of the States for un-American activities, because he was a left winger. He ran away to Europe.

Sam used to call me Margi – with a soft 'G' not hard 'G' – but he was too old to correct.

I started to tell Mr Fuller the story of Blonde Fist, and then he asked me what the title was.

I told him 'Raging Cow'. He took a big puff on his cigar, blew out a load of smoke and said: "Blonde Fist...you are the Blonde Fist".

The reason he gave me the title was it reminded him of a famous Film Noir movie he'd made called The Big Red One.

The first scene of Blonde Fist showed my character's father bare-knuckle fighting in the back yard of a pub, and at the same time his wife is giving birth on top of a sack of budgie millet in a stall in Kirkby.

It was life and death.

Sam also told me the same theme opened The Big Red One – the opening scene was a battlefield in the First World War, with death and destruction everywhere, and at the same time there's a woman giving birth. That's why he responded the way he did, because the story of Blonde Fist put the same images into his mind, and he generously came up with a brilliant title.

Frank had immediately started writing and he had the script ready in a couple of weeks. This was also Frank's directorial debut, and he wanted to make sure he had control of the cast, because he'd had problems over casting with The Fruit Machine. He wanted to make sure that it was really well tuned, and at the beginning there was almost a chance of a two million pound budget.

Almost a chance...

That amount of money, for us, would have been pure luxury. That would have given us the opportunity to execute the dream, while having the ability to pay for the best to do it. And Frank was always brilliant at connecting things up.

But we made the film. The problem that we had in terms of casting was that there were no other actresses who could box, or who were prepared to learn how to box. So we had to go to real women boxers, for me to fight in the film.

I remember, in the first fight I had in the film, Frank made my opponent wear two big pigtails on either side of her head, so she looked daft. And the poor girl couldn't quite get the choreography right because, of course, you don't make contact. She walked straight onto my fist and got knocked out.

I was supposed to knock her out in the film, but it was real. To get the role right, I was training with Paul Hodkinson. That was a stroke of genius to have him involved, because at that time he was on the verge of becoming featherweight champion of the world. He was a classic Kirkby lad – really shy – but a brilliant, dedicated athlete. I trained with him in Kirkby stadium, which is no longer there. A lot of boxers had used that stadium.

Christopher Figg was one of the producers trying to secure the finance for the film. He was a bit of a 'Queen's guard type' and a decent fella, we all got on with him. The deal was almost done, I think it was with Harvey Weinstein or someone, but then something happened that wasn't supposed to happen – the first Gulf War. That completely lashed the finances and it took a while to get the money.

Of course, we had to use our imagination to make certain parts in the film happen. That was the case with the famous end scene. In the script of Blonde Fist, Ronnie O'Dowd had won the fight, she's got the belt and she's coming back to Liverpool in style on the QE2 with her father.

Needless to say, we couldn't afford to hire the QE2 for a day, so what did we do? Frank found a way around that.

He got a film crew together on a day when the QE2 was coming freely down the Mersey – all the Scousers were out for that, it was six-deep at the Pier Head against the railings – and worked it in with scenes of Ronnie and her father, who was played by Pete Postlethwaite. It worked well and provided a fantastic climax to the movie.

'Michael Douglas

came over and said:

"I think your movie

is fantastic. I think you're

fantastic . . . what do you think

about oral sex?"

I said: "No thank you, I like to

lick my own."

And with that he ordered

champagne'

11. Lasting Impressions

There were nine of us including our Frank and Angela, all staying in this really small apartment. We didn't have beds, we strung together some sanitary towels to sleep on, it was that tight for space. But it gave us the opportunity to do the Cannes Film Festival – on the cheap.

We were there to do some promotional work, but while I was in Cannes I was also working as a correspondent for Avant, a low budget magazine, and was primed to interview a major celebrity at the Hotel Ducape, which is where anyone 'who is anyone' stays.

It is about £25 by taxi from Cannes and is set in the most beautiful part of the coast; in fact, Ducape means 'Paradise rock'. The hotel consists of around 10 acres of villas set within a huge complex – and is absolute mayhem in terms of security.

About 500 guards surround the place but I'd got my press pass out of the 5,000 journalists all fighting for interviews back in town.

I was the most unlikely-looking journalist you will ever see, decked out in dark glasses and new age gear borrowed from my sister Angela. I'd gone along with an industry friend, John Nicholson, for support, who would help us out with public relations and is used to this sort of thing.

After negotiating the security and doing another interview I had planned, we were swanning around the hotel and suddenly this huge white schooner pulls up in the boat-packed bay. Full sails blasting and a gold bird on the top of the mast – I think it's the Liver Bird for a minute but that only ever flies as far as Birkenhead. Around two hundred people disembark onto the jetty leading to the hotel and every one of them is dressed twenties style, like something out of The Great Gatsby; all dicky-dolled up.

And I'm thinking, 'where's the cameras?'

They MUST be filming it.

But no, this wasn't part of a film, although it was part of an act. This was what the rich do. With their excess money, they can afford to play out some of the most fashionable time warps in the world. They live their lives in imaginary time capsules, waltzing around in period clothes whenever it suits them.

The kind of people I am talking about are the mega rich who sit in goats' milk – the heads of Warner Brothers and the other studios or the heads of your big organisations like Coca-Cola.

So me and John are there on the balcony taking the piss out of them wondering if they dress at Kumar's clothes shop because I have, when I notice a load of tables about 30 feet away, and people sat having after-noon tea.

That's when I see Michael Douglas.

It was about four years before when I had last met him. I was in New York to promote Letter to Brezhnev and I went to a club called Elaine's with Alexandra Pigg. We were both caked out of our brains on vodka because our nerves had gone, and Michael Douglas came over and said: "I think your movie is fantastic. I think you're fantastic...what do you think about oral sex?"

I said: "No thank you, I like to lick my own."

And with that he ordered champagne.

We were nattering away and he didn't understand my accent. In fact, he enjoyed me saying: "This means that...or whatever." At one point I turned round and said: "Do you mind if I mention your da'?" because I knew it might be a sensitive subject.

And he said: "What's my 'da'?"

I told him it meant his father, and his face clouded over. I think it was at the time when he'd had a bit of trouble in that direction, but he said: "No, go right ahead."

I just went: "De derrr de...De derrr de' and Alex joined in.

And the two us were just sat there singing the theme from The Vikings because, for most people, that and Spartacus were his father's image. Alexandra and me were giving it loads, screaming and laughing. We never got on to rape and pillage, but it was a fabulous night.

So years later I'm stood on this balcony in the Ducape looking at him wearing his gorgeous blue silky suit that could have been a Giorgio Armani, but I'm sure he's got more taste.

I'm thinking, 'Right, Margi girl, gather up all your psychic power and make him look up at YOU.'

Unfortunately, I'm not that psychic or that powerful and anyway, it would have meant him doing a 360-degree turn with his head like something out of The Exorcist – I didn't want to frighten him at this stage. Instead, I go down to him, floating past the commissionaires on the door.

With my dark glasses on, unbeknown to me, it must have appeared to Michael Douglas that I was Glenn Close from Fatal Attraction, because I walk up to him and say: "Hi ya, Michael, how are you, lad?" the way you do.

And he looks up at me and says: "I'm fine. Who are you?"

Lifting my glasses, I screech: "Don't you remember me? Margi Clarke from Letter to Brezhnev? Don't you remember when you told me in Elaine's about oral sex?"

The Hollywood suits at the table start tittering.

He stares at me and says: "Well, Margi, it's one thing talking about oral sex in New York and another thing to talk about oral sex around the table in Cannes."

For a second I think I've blown it, but recover in time to say: "What can you do when your wellies let in?" I re-gather my composure (and the violin that is bound to come out) and really go for it...

"You see, Michael, I've got this mate in Liverpool called Smokey and he's on the bones of his arse.

"He's got this little magazine called Avant and it was his lifetime's ambition to come to Cannes and converse with the stars, but he could-n't afford the aeroplane ticket, so I said that I'd do it for him. And this actor, who's a megastar, RoboCop, has just given me this fab interview."

He said: "Well, Margaret, I'd like to give you a fab interview, too."

He looks up to see my intrepid friend, John, surrounded by a cluster of cameras on the overhead balcony and freaks out – once again.

"No, no. Not on camera. Not on camera."

"Simmer down, Michael lad, I just found them in the pub," I reassure him.

So we arrange a time and a place.

I retreat to the ladies room and dig out – from my lipsticks – the last remains of vermillion red. I never go anywhere without my bits. Now, greased in confidence, I'm ready for the Master of the Universe. Meanwhile, the cock-eyed stare of John, posted on the balcony, watch-es the Master's every move.

Some time passes and Michael gets up to leave his table.

I leg it downstairs and grab him before some other floozy gets her nails into him.

"COOOO-OOOOO-EEEEEY!"

He walks towards me and I'm thinking: 'Is this my last chance to be a groupie in room 302, or will Jamie's love and my press badge win the day?'

But there was no need for such filth anyway as Michael, the perfect gentleman, guides my sunburnt sausage arms out to the garden, where only a chirping cuckoo breaks the bliss.

He knows that I'm not a journalist, and I think that's what entertains him more than anything.

I tell him I've just done a film with a Finnish director called Aki

Kaurismaki.

"Aki Kaurismaki sounds like a Japanese whore house," he laughs.

"It's called I Hired a Contract Killer. I've just done that and my brother's going to direct me in Blonde Fist, where I play a female boxer."

"Fantastic," he says. "And your brother's directing?"

"Yeah, he wrote Letter to Brezhnev."

"I know that. He's a director?"

We'll let that one go...

"Frank was the writer..." I continue. "I was telling him how I met you for the first time in Elaine's and it's been my party piece ever since: 'How I met Michael Douglas.'"

I carried on.

"Michael, you said to me you loved Letter to Brezhnev."

He said: "I did, I loved the whole concept.

"The writing's fantastic, you were extraordinary and it just had a lyricism I have not seen in a long time."

I push. "It announced the end of the Cold War, didn't it?"

He agrees. "I thought so. For the first time, too. You're right."

I push again

"You're a bit left wing yourself, aren't you, Michael?"

He agrees: "I think so. My politics tend to be more socialist."

I say: "Good on ya, kid."

"I guess so, yeah, you know it was the way I was brought up.

"I realise now that my stepfather was part of the Communist party in the forties and my father Kirk was the first person to hire Dalton Trumbo, you know, who did the screenplay for Spartacus under his real name after the black-listing.

"So yeah, life's been good to me and I try, at least in spirit and hopefully financially, to share it to some degree with other people.

"Yeah," he reiterates.

I ask him how his socialist principles come into practice and he tells me that he's backing a newspaper in Los Angeles – "because our papers are quite like your papers. They ARE the government. Their views are what everyone listens to because there's so many TV networks that it's hard to get a good opinion. So people cull it from a newspaper. I thought I'd put money into the LA Weekly.

"For 10 years it didn't make a cent, but I wasn't upset by that.

"I wanted to be able to put our view of the world; I wanted to put my money into that type of project."

I'm impressed and love him more by the minute.

I tell him that not only is he a good actor, but that the gods must like him because he's got the gift.

"Well, thank you," he responds – modestly.

He goes on: "I don't know if I have a gift. I think YOU have a gift. But I've worked really hard.

"I was not somebody who naturally liked performing. I used to have a wastebasket and, in my university plays, I would puke every time before I went on stage. And for years I was terrified of a camera.

"In fact, it was the television series Streets of San Francisco which just got me used to being in front of a camera a lot, you know. I mean, they could make these cameras look a lot nicer, like put carpets over them or paint pictures on them – they always looked like X-ray machines in my dentists' office."

Michael Douglas...scared of cameras?

"Well, they are quite spooky" I respond, turning to his last movie with Kathleen Turner.

"You mean War of the Roses?"

"Yeah, you seem to be doing a lot of work with Katherine." (See, I'm not a journalist.)

"Kathleen," he corrects.

I think he can tell I haven't seen War of the Roses but he lets it go, like I didn't pick him up on Frank's directing – all part of the interview/interviewee etiquette, you know.

"Kathleen. Well, that just happened that way. We did two films –

Romancing the Stone and The Jewel of the Nile – and Danny DeVito, who was my oldest friend, he and I got our first acting job together in 1965 – the first time they paid you money to act and you could call yourself a professional.

"So when Danny offered me the part in The War of the Roses I wanted to do it, and when we started talking about a leading lady, of course, Kathleen came up. Danny and Jim Brookes himself – an Academy award-winning director and writer who produced the movie – were nervous of Kathleen.

"It came out of the Romancing series. But I thought that I should be helped, because as sick as Roses was, it was nice if you had a familiarity with the characters. So the truth of the matter is that there was not a lot of leading ladies who could do that – and she's a wonderful actress."

"She's very good looking – isn't she?"

"She's pretty good looking – nice jams."

Nice jams. For a minute I think he's talking about jam butties, but I'm sure he means tits.

"What are you like, eh?"

I laugh and steer the subject back to backgrounds.

I offer that people are inclined to think that Michael Douglas's dad has got a few bob.

"Well, I certainly didn't starve," he retorts, "but on the other hand there was not any big trust fund or anything like that. I think the biggest problem, I mean, he was very supportive throughout college, but the biggest problem is that when you've got a father who has such a strong identity and is popular as he was, it was always a question of 'how can I ever be the man my father is?'

"And I think that their mothers subjugate a lot of people too – that a lot of children suffer what happens. That suffering is a part of life – just dealing with the struggle of 'how can I be close to the man my father was?' But my father was extremely supportive. He sat in at a play I did in college.

"He was convinced he had nothing to worry about – that I would never become an actor. And the gift for me came from somewhere that I don't understand.

"I think it was this hippie thing in the '60s, when they never made any commitments about anything and nothing was straight 24 hours a day, that I found this work ethic which...I don't really know."

"It might have been the bad brown acid Michael", I said.

"I wouldn't know about that. I think that the only thing that's most misunderstood about my career and my work is how hard I've actually worked. I get angry and defensive when people forget that. It's been 20 years." (It was 1990 at the time.)

Just as I am about to ask Michael my next question, a fellow inmate walks past and bids him good day.

I have a sense that time is running out.

I ask: "Does your love of work, Michael, come from the Jewish work ethic?"

"My father is Jewish," he answers, "and at 73 still lifting weights. But the work ethic also comes from my mother.

"My parents' love of the theatre is how they met. My mother was at school on the Isle of Wight in England and when she was 16-years-old she lied about her age and went to the American Academy of Dramatic Arts, where she met this Russian Jewish peasant guy, Issur Demsky, my father the ragman's son. The two of them are so different."

It's a natural language that's moulded the charisma of Michael Douglas.

His entourage, meanwhile, are ready to head off and drag him and his charisma away. But before he goes I suggest doing a movie together.

"I'd have to find a script," he says.

"Even if it is only conversations about oral sex. I'd love it. You leave a lasting impression, Miss Clarke."

I think, as I watch the blue suit flapping up the hill that America, like the Hotel Ducape, is drawing more and more into itself – it's only making movies about its own idyllic bubble.

But Hollywood isn't a place – it's a time in the forties and that time is gone. It would be cleverer if America took its stars out of the little countries to find new stories. Burt Lancaster tuned into it with Local Hero.

So, maybe, it's not that far-fetched for Michael to work with a girl from the third world. We could call our movie Lasting Impressions.

"Don't forget, Michael now," I shout after him.

"It's Clarke with an E."

I wasn't afraid to approach the big Hollywood stars. After all, I was in the same profession – why not? She who dares...

I have always been hard-faced.

As I watched Michael Douglas walk away, my mind drifted back to the time when I met the one and only Jack Nicholson.

I was in a film called Strike It Rich, based on Graham Greene's novel Loser Takes All. I was playing the role of Nurse, which involved pushing Max Wall around in a wheelchair.

It was filmed at Pinewood, that lovely studio in the countryside at Borehamwood.

They had a 1960s-style cafeteria and who do I see but Jack Nicholson, over in the UK on pre-production for Batman. I watched him wolf down his breakfast and hold forth at the same time with a couple of men in suits.

I so much wanted to go over in my nurse's uniform and introduce myself. But for the first time I didn't have the bottle. I was disappointed with myself when I returned from lunch and grouped up, talking on the set waiting for the camera to turn over.

For some mad reason I made up a whopper.

I told the lovely Frances de la Tour, the multi-talented star who became a household name thanks to Rising Damp (and who was also appearing in the film) that I had, indeed, gone over to Jack in the canteen and said "hello".

Frances looked horrified.

"But my dear", she said. "Jack is royalty."

I felt ashamed I'd spun Frances a lie. I decided there and then that I was going to find Jack Nicholson, and make the falsehood come true.

Eventually, I found him in a massive studio the size of an aircraft hangar. I spied him through the glass panel in the heavy door sitting on what can best be described as a prop throne, indeed the royalty status Frances had mentioned. He was on the stage of Tim Burton's upcoming Batman movie.

I had already rehearsed what I would say to Jack and, as I pulled open the reluctant door with the air of a nurse on a mission, I walked across the studio floor and looked directly at him.

I swear it was like looking at a nuclear bomb about to be launched.

His intelligent eyebrows were raised as I held out my hand and introduced myself.

"Sister Margaret here, Jack.

"I hear you are having trouble with yer knob."

Quick as a flash, the legendary actor from The Shining (which I hadn't seen at this point or if I had, I would never have gone near him) shot back:

"Well, sister Margaret.

"It could do with a bit of spit and polish..."

'That TV programme was the equivalent of Madonna. We brought sex out into the open, while she sold the subject on the coffee tables of the world. This was real sex appeal.'

12. Sex Goddess

After Blonde Fist, I was just finishing on Making Out – coming to the end of the second series – when I got invited to see the producers of a new show to be made by Carlton TV called The Good Sex Guide.

The plan was for a series of half-hour programmes going out on the ITV network at around 10.35 in the evening.

The entertaining purpose of the show was to help improve peoples' sex lives, while getting the message across in a new, funny way. The programme would have a main presenter and then feature some humourous, light-hearted sketches, often starring guest celebrities.

It was a bold project for the time. This was 1991 and there had never been such a programme on mainstream television.

When they showed me the breakdown for the subject matter of the series, I was intrigued how they were going to put all the research together.

They were very interested in me as a presenter and I'd heard that Kim Wilde, the sexy singer-turned gardening programme-maker, had been offered it so there was Kim and I in the frame.

I think what really got me the part was that I had presented on telly before. All that training I got from the Margox years worked to my advantage. It was like a returning career cycle. Presenting direct to camera wasn't a new experience for me, but no one was aware of the on-screen training I'd received at Granada Television.

I went down to see Vicky Barras, a posh but switched-on producer who also worked with me on a series called Swank – a proto-type copy for Trinny and Susannah. Swank was me and the lovely David Emanuel as co-presenters. David was renowned as the man who 'built' Princess Diana's frock. It as the height of Daytime TV and Swank was a commission that fitted the bill for the type of light afternoon shows that were taking off. It was another mould-breaker.

Vicky was keen on me for The Good Sex Guide but Jamie and I had just had Rowan, our daughter, and I thought that might prove a bit of a practical problem. She was only six weeks old. In the end it was no trouble at all. I took Rowan on the job with me. In between scenes, I was breast-feeding and she was dragged from pillar-to-post, location to location as we filmed. She was with me and I was nursing her.

Rowan's always been so special to me. She came along after I had suffered one of the most upsetting episodes in my life.

It all started one morning when I got up for an audition in London. I was in pain – the worst pain I had ever been in. I was crawling around the bed, vomiting. I actually passed a clot, but instead of going back to bed I continued on to the audition.

I wasn't feeling with it, and needless to say I didn't get the part.

After I came out I collapsed, and ended up getting taken to the University Hospital. They told me that I had had a miscarriage – that it had been an ectopic pregnancy and that they'd have to take my Fallopian tubes away. I begged them not to. I said: "No, I want to leave this life with all my bits intact, is there anything else you can do?"

So they left them – but they said I was unlikely to get pregnant again because my Fallopian tubes were too scarred, and then, hey presto, I became pregnant with Rowan not long after that. So after all that, Rowan became extra special to me.

My mam also helped me out on the set of The Good Sex Guide with Rowan. I would take the favourite route of all Scouse mothers: "Nanna – where's my Nanna?"

My mother was brilliant – absolutely fantastic. She took care of Rowan for me and she would help with any guilt that I had about being a mother and legging it off to London – doing 50 hours a week, maybe more with travelling on top of it.

She said: "Look, girl. When I was a little girl we saw our mother one day a week because she went off with the hand cart.

"My grandma pushed that cart for 50 years to Marsh Lane six-days-a-week and she left at half four in the morning and came in at six o'clock at night...exhausted.

"So you go and do it and make sure Rowan has a good education."

I had that support and Jamie and me were really very happy. He was brilliantly tolerant. He never ever made me feel like I was embarrassing him or the family doing The Good Sex Guide.

Jamie and I had been involved in a big campaign protesting against Clause 28, which basically banned local authorities or schools from promoting homosexuality.

The Good Sex Guide was set against the backdrop of those times. I lost a lot of my friends through HIV – quite a few from Liverpool and also from the film world. At the time there was a government propaganda campaign that was terrifying the life out of everyone about AIDS. The Tories even wanted to ban kids' favourite 'Noddy' because they thought he was gay.

So here I was, not knowing where my next piece of acting work was coming from and I was being asked to present a show that was pretty controversial. It was right up my straza.

What I liked about it from the outset was that it broke new ground – nothing like that had ever been on the telly before. It had great production values and had a few bob behind it, too. It had the support of the medical profession but it wasn't just another sex education programme. It was the first upfront sex education show.

It had lots of entertainment, and good comedy scripts. Richard Curtis, who went on to write Notting Hill, wrote a lot of these clever sketches –

we called them 'Arty Fuck Shots' and there were plenty of them.

As well as seeing what I could do on screen, I believe they went for me as a presenter because I always gave good interviews. I think my interviews in the press had some value for me, then. I always gave good copy – I always gave good headlines. I understood that we're all in it together. That may have helped.

I used to say some outrageous things in the press – I'd just let it rip. My mum used to say: "Margi, why can't you be more like Judi Dench?"

Having said that, when the series went out I didn't want me mam to see it. That made the papers as a story in its own right.

I wasn't the only one who was a bit wary of how I'd come across on screen in such a controversial programme. The show also interviewed members of the public and all the people who appeared in The Good Sex Guide said the same thing: "Oh, what if me mu   m and dad see it?"

I was no different to them. I used to say: "Look, I've got the cloak of invisibility here and it's wrapped around you because your mother won't say YOU are 'a mucky pup', she would say: 'Isn't that Margi Clarke a saucy mare?'" That's what it was in a way – me acting as a lightning rod.

The programme went out on a Friday night and I used to box me mother off with money for the bingo – so she wouldn't be in front of the telly when I was on. But of course she still got to hear all about it. She used to get back from the bingo hall and tell me what they'd been saying about me. Apparently there was this one woman who always complained about me on The Good Sex Guide and my mother said: "Look...it's not the Good Gardening Report...or the Good Weather Report. If you don't like it – turn it off. Turn over."

Although the pace was furious and I was a nursing mum, I loved making it. I could put all the skills I'd learned into play. It was clever. It all stemmed from an idea from two Welsh fellas, I think. Their remit was education programmes. So that is where the budget came from – educational sources. Good, informative television.

What they managed to do was instead of it coming out as something you would read in print, hear on radio or on telly, say, connected to the NHS (that type of feel like a public education message) well, they actually wrapped it all up in plenty of showbiz.

They had the likes of Helena Bonham Carter playing some of the sketches. Timothy Spall, too, was in it and a long list of performers included Men Behaving Badly stars (behaving very funnily early on) Neil Morrissey and Martin Clunes; Blackadder's Baldrick Tony Robinson; EastEnders' Leslie Grantham and Young Ones' star Nigel Planer – just a few amongst many household names.

The way they shot the series, well, really, the public were the real stars. They were massive in the picture frame and had nice, big close-ups and excellent lighting. And when you threw all that in the mix and you had the arty fuck shots, it was a real huge ratings-winner. We had created something unbelievable – about 13 million viewers tuned in at one point.

I did three series and the third was The Good Sex Guide Abroad. I went to France, Italy, Germany and over to Canada and to Malaysia. Not a bad job – it was an excellent time.

The show was high profile and I was in demand and able to do some one-off specialist programmes in between recording.

One was a TV programme called Mystic Challenge where a woman, who was a psychic, had to find out who I, the mystery guest, was.

I was wearing a big cloak on me head and I think she thought I was Frank Bruno with this hood. I wasn't allowed to reveal who I was because, if I did, it would have been 'game up.'

This psychic talked about life regressions and she asked me if I knew how many lives I'd had?

I said, joking: "Oh, about 9,000."

She said: "Yes, you have had 9,999."

I said: "I knew I was a greedy bitch – but not that greedy."

She said: "Some people have millions of lives."

After the show was in the can, the psychic lady was gabbing about life regressions.

Anyway, having just done The Good Sex Guide, it was interesting to hear of three special past lives I'd had according to her.

I was a nun twice...

My name is Margaret Mary Bernadette Clarke and I took myself off to extra Catholic tuition at the age of eight. So, when she told me that I'd gone into religious orders, I said: "Yeah I can see that," and was then told that I had been an Abbotess – Head Nun.

She also said I was once a peasant nun with fantastic faith.

Then, finally, I was also Liverpool's premier prostitute...Maggie May. Now, when I look back on it, I think about my interest in that character and realise that I had been Maggie May – I am Maggie May.

There was a sort of connection because doing The Good Sex Guide, in a brilliant way, was like being a sex fertility goddess.

There weren't many down sides – or any big negative aspects.

For a while, instead of 'Film star Margi Clarke' now I was referred to as 'The Good Sex Guide presenter'. That tag – from that moment on – came with everything I did.

It took until Coronation Street to get my 'actress' credits and tag lines back.

There were some other downers. After the series everyone thought they could talk to ME about SEX. I am claustrophobic and I don't like to feel I am over-powered – not knowing my way out – like being in a taxi, that type of thing. Before The Good Sex Guide, taxi drivers would never have normally engaged me in a conversation about sex but after it they did. I didn't like talking about it in taxis and situations like that. I didn't really mind it anywhere else. If it was late at night and I was on my own and trapped in a car with someone, well, put yourself in that position – you wouldn't because it's bad manners.

I left myself reluctantly open to it because I was – in their eyes – now a pundit on sex.

The other negative aspect was that it did – temporarily – effect my sex life. It was like working in a cake shop, a bit like a scenario where if you shove one more cake in – there's no more room for anymore.

And if you were talking about it all the time – you'd gabbed it all out your system.

But I would say The Good Sex Guide was probably a pinnacle of my career because it got everyone talking – it wasn't just something you watched on the telly and forgot. It was something that loads of people were busy doing at the time of watching it. I said to myself: 'I wonder if there are new Margi Clarkes around?'

It had a massive effect. People talked about the programme the next morning in work and they discussed it on the back of the bus.

When you consider at that time we were a tight-lipped country – the stiff upper wasn't on the upper anymore.

It was a good time in my life. It had an incredible effect because it was right for the culture of the time.

It took a really grown-up look at sexuality and many aspects for young people who didn't have a clue about sex and who were raring to go – they were chomping at the bit. They could now talk about it because it was good television – was well researched – 100 per cent top marks. I was learning things about sex, too. I was picking up tips and gaining an insight into what makes men tick.

The show helped me understand the great motivations with men, because men don't ask much and it's not something women will openly talk about – but will as a group.

I learned things about fella's and their PC muscle – the one at the back of his 'town halls' – if he squeezes the magic PC muscle it stops his orgasm.

I didn't think I knew everything but I thought I was open-minded enough and I don't get embarrassed that easy by sex – equivalent to a nurse not being scared by blood. It was just a natural calmness I've got. I call it earthiness.

I have some great memories about filming The Good Sex Guide.

One of the highlights was when they took me to this rugby club in

Yorkshire. There were all these proper fit broad fella's. They all had fantastic shoulders. I love broad-shouldered men.

I was given the best vantage point ever to look at and judge a man's penis, not staring down from above but lying on the floor in the changing rooms.

I was lying there with a red rubber dress on, like I'd been poured into it (my figure post-baby was fab) and all these testosterone-fuelled men were standing over me.

And from THAT position I had a bird's eye view on a fella's manhood – every cock in the house looked frigging enormous.

When you are looking down on something it's hardly there, but when you are looking up...it doesn't half fill your eyeballs.

I discovered that men love visuals. If I'd have gone into that changing room wearing my chicken stuffer's outfit from Letter to Brezhnev I doubt they would have groaned in desire – no matter which way I was looking at them. That episode was about giving men confidence – illustrating that size doesn't matter.

That said, I terrified the life out of the fella's I was with – winding them up, especially when they saw me with a tape measure.

I said: "Look, lads, don't worry. I don't measure them. I weigh them."

They were well up for it – young, fit men and I was at my prime. I had to detach myself from one attraction – a room full of steaming men, very exciting work. It wasn't pornography, well, maybe, 'light or soft'. It was a valuable, great way to take in the message of the show. That sort of British prudishness that we are known for, well, I'm happy it blew that right out of the water, and it came with real information for people.

I did notice at one point that the output – emphasis – was put on men's sex lives and I wondered what could we do for women?

Gordon, one of five researchers, found out that more than half of all women didn't have an orgasm. I was gobsmacked and appalled that so many women were going without such a given pleasure.

I said to the producers: "We have to teach women to have an orgasm."

Then they picked actress Caroline Langrishe from Lovejoy to present that one. She was a posh version of me.

I am proud that Britain made that programme.

One of the countries that lapped it up was also known as a prudish place – Canada. Apparently, in Canada, it ended up being debated in their parliament – it caused that much furore.

When I went out there to promote it they rolled out the red carpet. It was great. I was on everything – radio, TV, all the media. I loved being able to communicate and get a message over.

I was even interviewed by 'Fred the Talking Sock' on a cult Canadian puppet show called The Good Sock Guide. It was late-night TV and I said to him: "I've come to sock you off."

What I learnt from The Good Sex Guide was that men get turned on by visuals – a pair of suspenders, stilettos and frilly, sexy things – but that doesn't do much for a woman.

What does it for a woman is the words of love.

Words.

Aural sex, yes and oral sex...and laughter is essential for women.

We did a show on chat-up lines. I'd be out and about asking the public: "Where is the clitoris?" We did this item called 'Pin the clitoris on the donkey'. It used to end up on the donkey's head.

I was happy then and well off. I still call it living in the 'Wonder Years'. I was never off the train to London – 'Box Car Bertha' they called me, she rides the train with panache. A sign of success as a few years before I'd been bunking them.

It was an exciting time and I was firing on all cylinders. I'd been with Jamie for about 16 years and I was at my most stable – a fantastic period in my life. I was at my happiest.

'People were outraged by one of my stand-up props. It was a ten foot, blow-up portable cock. "Bloody hell", I thought, "get over it"'

13. Soul Survivor

I was ready to go out there, do my own stuff. Granted, written by our Frank. But a show that would tear down the accepted things in stand-up. I'd worked with Jamie Reid on the on-going collective package of Leaving The 21st Century, and this was a stand-up show with a difference.

The time was right, the script was ready and we went out on the road. I suppose the audience wasn't ready – we got hammered.

But we enjoyed it. The reviewers didn't.

My Carleen, Frank and Jamie were all terrified that if I read the reviews of my stand-up show 21st Century Scutt that I'd put on my coat and go home.

But I programmed it – that the show must go on. The battle still had to commence. But the press raged against it.

I always wanted to push the boundaries, try new things. A stand-up show was a natural progession.

On the opening night our Carleen and a pal were with me in a taxi trying to coach me. They were doing one of those exercises from my Everyman Youth Theatre days saying, "We are strong. We are strong." And we kept on repeating it. Then I walked on stage – that was the scariest. But the money was already in the bank.

It's that first 10 minutes – or seconds – that matter when you're up there on stage all on your own. With any live situation, get it right and you've got your audience. You can go ahead – it's crucial.

But according to the reviews 21st Century Scutt was a flop.

It was written by Frank for me and was a mixture of stand-up observations and monologues. It was a man writing for a woman but with a lot of improv – Frank gave me scope to go off on tangents within the structure. It caused uproar. I remember one sketch aimed at men.

"What is the difference between a pub and the clitoris?"

Answer: "Men will always find the pub."

Yet it was really funny for all the wrong reasons. It was an event on its own. People were outraged by one of my props, a 10-foot inflatable cock. 'Bloody hell' I thought, 'get over it. It's just an inflatable, portable cock.' While I was on stage doing the opening bits of the tales, it looked like a big discarded piece of crimplene – like a bit of fabric. It was there on the stage, but you sort of forgot about it – it was just left there because you didn't know what it was.

As I progressed with the show, there was a fan underneath it and it started to come up and get bigger and bigger and wallop yer in the gob when it came to its full height.

I wanted the men in the audience to come on to ride the cock. Because I thought, well, women know how to ride cocks – but do men?

It's great that it came out – the show that is. It taught me about things you could get away with – what's viable and what isn't.

My first love is acting – that's the most challenging. Then I love singing – I've always been a dilettante – I'm even a potter. I like to turn my hand to anything.

I'm a good all-rounder and it's difficult for the business to understand that. Music, poetry, art, presenting...I will give it all a go.

I wouldn't mind doing An Audience with Margi Clarke around the country now. I am older and wiser. I have the vast experience and when it comes to show business, I've been through the wash house haven't I? Everything is exposed by the time you get to where I am. There isn't much by this stage that you don't know yourself.

I do think mistakes are helpful when it comes to a career. You don't learn anything from licking a lolly ice on a beach. You learn it all from things that test you – that's what brings us out and helps us to evolve.

So when it comes to reviews I take them in. I do read reviews because I am an avid reader. I really do read everything I can get my hands on.

All my friends were scared I was going to run away and leave because of the critics. They thought that any other actress would put a scarf on, cover her head and do a runner.

Looking back I still laugh at the experience of Scutt. I toured with it after its premiere at the Everyman in Liverpool, and played the Royal Festival Hall in Edinburgh.

On the first night in Edinburgh there was a heckler in the audience – a real professional heckler. So I'd already had bad reviews and now I've got to deal with a heckler.

So I ignored her.

Anyway, halfway through the show I have to decide what to do – pass the whole show to this heckler, or carry on with what I am supposed to be doing. I decided the best course of action was to blank her and keep doing the show.

So when we get to the end and she's up in the gods and just after I've taken a bow, I shout up to her: "See yer, luv. You're getting the end of my stilleto up the crack of yer arse."

It was a classic line from our Frank.

People had also been fighting in the audience on either aisle – there was a big barney. Punters were shouting for and and against my show, others were getting escorted out. It was bedlam in there...there was no order – it became a creative free-for-all.

The audience were split like a Manx kipper right down the middle – some loved it. Others thought it was the biggest pile of shite they'd ever seen.

But we did it and some liked it hot. Others turned cold.

Back in the dressing room there was this woman from the BBC and I was trying to get myself calmed down after what had been a difficult experience. So I did the interview with the BBC woman from Radio 4 in my dressing room, which was fine. Then we go downstairs to the bar and she says: "I'll get you a drink," so she gets me an orange with soda.

The next thing is, a woman turns around and says: "There she is..." and there was this heckler. The BBC woman had set me up for it.

I waltzed over to the heckler, and said: "Excuse me, love" or "excuse me, dear.

"I told you I'd be down here to put the end of my stiletto up the crack of your arse, and better still take a swilling."

Then I threw the glass of orangeade in her gob.

I felt terrible after I'd done it – what a really terrible thing to do, I thought, because the poor woman's contact lens was sitting on her cheek. She then said to me – dripping in orangeade (and in a high-pitched voice): "But I didn't go to your show, I've been to see Roger McGough." Following that incident the production company had to give away 500 free tickets just to appease the woman.

Anyway, I'd just finished The Good Sex Guide in around 1995 and I was with a really good agent called Lou Coulson. She got on the phone to me and said one day: "We've got a great part for you, darling, it's going to be shot in Liverpool and it's going to be featuring fab actors – including Ian McShane."

In Soul Survivors I was playing a character that was slightly out of my class, for the first time. I wasn't typecast, as I normally am but then as I always say, as long as you are cast, that's the main thing.

I was playing a secretary who was quite flirtatious. I was cast slightly out of character for me and wearing a honey blonde wig. I portrayed the personal assistant with more reserve but still plenty of charm.

I was a bit nervous of Ian McShane – I'd never really watched telly; I never really watched Lovejoy, which is what he's most famous for to many people, and I thought he might be a bit 'smarmy'. I thought he was going to be a terrible Tory, but he wasn't. He really surprised me.

It can happen like that sometimes, when you have a preconceived opinion of what someone is going to be like and then you meet them and you get a surprise.

Ian had respect for everyone on the set and I loved that. I've worked with people who are disrespectful – not to me – but to the make-up artist or to the wardrobe, and it makes me cringe. Ian has massive presence. He's only small, so much so that me and him could see eye-to-eye, but he behaved like a star should. He also came across as a real family man – he loved talking about his wife.

I gave him a painting, which Jamie had done, called 'How To Become Invisible'. It had been one of my poems originally which Jamie had turned into a painting. Ian loved that.

Don't be mistaken, though. I didn't fancy him – I never fancy actors. The press always got it wrong about me. I was promiscuous on-screen, but not off. Off-screen I was really stable.

I couldn't have done The Good Sex Guide if I'd been 'Girl About Town' – I'd have been all over the papers, they'd have soon got on to it. I was really happy with Jamie and Rowan in that period.

Soul Survivors was filmed in St John's Tower – another of the striking landmarks of Liverpool's skyline.

Liverpool landmarks draw me to them. I remember that for the city's launch of European Capital of Culture year in 2008, I was walking down the Dock Road. It was bitterly cold, the start of January. I was totally isolated and then out of the inky, black night came all these fireworks.

I went right down to the water's edge and I'm looking out into the darkness and the next thing I see is the arse end of a ship – a massive liner called The Corona – and who was on board the ship?

It was only the cast of Coronation Street. No Scousers on board... thank you very much.

I thought it was strange that there were no local celebrities involved. The politician John Prescott was on it, which I didn't mind because at least he was a seafarer.

But I felt that it was like the Liver Bird had got me out to see it, like she'd said: "Come on, Marg, you've got to get down there. This is a big event, you've got to see this." I was drawn to the Pier Head.

Another time I found myself walking down Hanover Street and I felt drawn to the old Casartelli Building. I crossed over to the derelict structure and peered through the crumbling walls. Immediately I felt transported through time to the days of the older Liverpool women, the Mary Ellens. I was transfixed. Then I read in the Echo that the building had fallen down the very next day. I was flabbergasted.

So being in Soul Survivors, and being up in the tower, was great. Because when we were kids it was somewhere that you always wanted to go up. The 'penis of Liverpool'. It made a fantastic radio station and later on, life imitated art when Radio City moved into it.

Soul Survivors was a great challenge for me because I was trying to use a different tone.

I was being careful because when I'd done I Hired A Contract Killer I tried to use a softer, more refined accent, and I'd asked my dad: "What d'you think", and he said: "You sound like a silent movie actress trying to make it into talkies." That was exactly like when we were kids and you were made to get up on the table on a Sunday afternoon – when he'd come back from the boozer and you were made to perform.

And, yes, it felt like he'd thrown another wet dishcloth in me gob.

I was delighted to take part in Soul Survivors where I was shown with a different aspect – I think it did alter peoples' perception of me...a little bit. When you're seen as only one type of performer, it was great to be given another chance to be seen as something different. I can be directed.

Ian McShane generously gave me more close-ups. That's where an actor is always giving them an ace, because when you are in 'close-up' you are totally in connection with the receiver, the audience.

Soul Survivors had such great actors in it, as well as Ian. There was Isaac Hayes and Antonio Fargas – most famous as Huggy Bear in the original TV series Starsky and Hutch. It had such an effect on Antonio that he moved over to Liverpool and lived here for seven years.

I loved Isaac – he was lovely. I also loved Shaft. That is one of the iconic Hollywood detective films. At the end of the wrap, on the final day we had an auction and sold off the props for charity. Isaac donated his silver electric blue jacket – it went for £52 so someone out there is wearing a piece of history. That was also the time that I used to go down to the Moonstone pub in Liverpool. A few of us used to go there after the day's filming. We all used to be wearing leather, and I had my Afro wig on. And there was Isaac.

I was watching how he was with other women. We were filming in Mags – a great little place on Seel Street, an old warehouse full of old-fashioned furniture, stuffed to the gills.

They were using the courtyard – the same location that we used for filming Blonde Fist – and one of the cleaners there was a little old woman called Dolly. She was only the size of a doll – I think the mop was bigger than her. Anyway, Isaac Hayes was flirting with her and she thought he was marvellous. She was lapping it up. I like that. It was a great atmosphere.

I also made a great friend in the crew – the runner on it, Ian Hoskins. We are best mates now.

Soul Survivors was about a radio presenter who's got this record by the Tallahassees and he loves them, so he goes over to the Deep South on the trail of the band. That was basically the story. When you look at the way history has gone since, and how Ian so successfully played the role of Al Swearengen in Deadwood, he helped to take Scouse swear words to America.

My mother came on the set of Soul Survivors and had a great time. She wasn't well then. Frances loved Ian – she loved Lovejoy, that was right up her street. My mother's bedroom was like Steptoe's yard – she'd get stuff from car boot sales and second-hand shops.

My dad used to tut: "Not more, Frances."

I came back and told her what a nice fella Ian was – he'd told me that he didn't mind paying tax and I thought at the time, there's someone with a lot of money who doesn't mind paying tax. That made me view him from a different side. The Tories were still in power then.

But Soul Survivors improved my professionalism. It developed me as an actress. I didn't look exactly like ME – they put a wig on me and a pair of glasses.

It was a soft, gentle touch.

I also tried to do that with The Good Sex Guide – I tried to soften parts of my voice because the subject matter was strong. When you're telling the nation about having sex for the first time, if I'd have been 'guttural' with it, it would have closed over. I didn't judge it – I never do – I was always massively grateful to be included.

'Roll up, roll up,
welcome to The Death and
Resurrection Show...
The Wilderness Years
written, directed, produced and
starring Margi Clarke.
Send in the clowns...
don't bother, I'm here'

14. Teeth

There is a time in some people's lives when they lose the plot. I lost my bearings – and worst of all, let go of my man.

Me splitting up with Jamie wasn't the only thing wrong in my life. Addiction was a shadow looming on the horizon.

I was about to lose everything – the corner stone of my life...my mum was dying of cancer.

She told us she had it six months earlier. We rallied as a family around my mam and willed her immune system to fight back.

But it already had a hold on Mam and the inevitable happened.

When my mam died...she died in my arms.

The pain and the grief was like a dig in the solar plexus; it was so awful. I couldn't face up to it. Afterwards, the rest of my family – my sisters and our Frank – got on with the grief and they accepted it.

I didn't.

I still think about her every day because when my mam was there all was well in the world. When you've got your mother, it's your happy days, but you don't even know it...

I had lots of money and all was well in the nest.

It was 1995 and I had just finished The Good Sex Guide Abroad Series.

I'd climbed the north face of the Eiger. I got there at last – my only trip up was over a mountain of cocaine. The next three years were about descent – each one dodgier than the last.

The first time I took it was in 1995.

I'd had spliffs before then, but I was never a heavy drinker despite what one tabloid paper said – that I was on two bottles of wine a day.

My mum was such a strong character, and she took up such a massive space in my life. Once that influence was removed, I was in the void. And once you're in the void, you don't know who the 'void riders' are going to be and you're left unprotected.

Liverpool was flooded with cocaine at that time – the whole town seemed to be addicted. It was an adopted pain killer. It was suddenly so easy to find – everyone was walking in the same shoes. They didn't flood Liverpool with counterfeit money – they did it with Class As.

Anything that you focus on you attract – I was focused on the wrong thing, served up by every dealer in town.

Cocaine had been a great advertisement from the seventies from Studio 51 – it had great press with stories of the beautiful people dabbing it on their noses like it was Max Factor. I became absorbed by it – it's mind controlling. I snorted it – it wasn't hard to find. For something that's illegal it was easy to get. It seemed like the coolest anaesthetic available.

I was still grieving for my mum when I took on the role of Tyrone's jailbird Mam, Jackie Dobbs, on Coronation Street in 1998. Even now it's on record that I don't think I played the part to the best of my ability.

I was off my cake.

I was still taking cocaine and it makes for a brittle performance. The critics didn't notice, the viewers didn't – but my family did.

So it was mum's death that triggered the downslide.

I loathe it. I think it's got an awful lot of people on 'mind control' and my mind was controlled by it. I used to call it 'THE WHITE WORM'. It burrows a hole in your personality and a big fat juicy worm comes out the other side – you're cooked, you're done.

I paid for EVERY single line I took. I paid handsomely over a period of time. I must have spent £20,000 on cocaine.

It was utterly selfish. My poor dad was so distraught, he was telling me to "fight back" and "come on, girl, get yourself off the floor."

Dad was standing over me telling me, like the boxing coach played by Burgess Meredith in Sly Stallone's Rocky in the original film: "COME ON GIRL, FIGHT BACK, get up off the floor and FIGHT back."

I was too exhausted to climb back in the ring. The toxins were taking a heavy toll on my body. I couldn't have been in a worse shape – but what stopped me in the end was that I got sick – and poverty helped.

It's hard for me to tell this part of the story because shame comes into it. Cocaine is such a destructive drug – your body suffers in so many different ways.

One of the biggest shocks for me came when I was walking along the road one day. It was windy. I became aware that my teeth were starting to feel loose – to shake. Not just one or two but my whole mouth.

I couldn't understand what was happening at first, but I came to understand that there are powerful, lethal chemicals in cocaine. Used consistently, this would contribute to the long-term shattering side effects of the drug.

Used over a period of time they can attack the bones in your mouth, and loosen your teeth by damaging the roots and gums. Now here I was, my poor teeth swaying in the breeze.

This appeared to be payback time for all the years of living dangerously and recklessly, shoving cocaine up my nose and ruining my nasal cavities and oral backbone.

I felt it was all too hard to take, I felt isolated but it was all of my own doing. Tragic.

I was at the lowest part of the cycle and I knew that the bounce back to good health and well-being could only be achieved by the 'put off for years' trip to the dentist. So I was booked in for an appointment anyone would fear, and feel sick at the very thought of. But it had to be done.

That dreaded Monday morning will always stay with me – the day my gob changed forever. My best friends – one on each arm – Lucy Dawson and Shaun McKenna walked with me to the 'peggie man', a great city dentist on the High Street.

I was the first appointment at 9am in the waiting room, which was empty. Shaun gave me a big, loving hug and escorted me into the 'Dentist's Den'.

I'd been worrying that once the blue clinging mouth mould set to my loose teeth, it would grip so tight that I feared my teeth would come out via the mould.

I asked the caring dentist if the mould would drag my teeth out.

He shuffled his feet nervously and looked away from me. I sensed a lot of pain would be involved, and pleaded for an anaesthetic.

I sat open-mouthed in disbelief when the dentist explained. "Margi, if I give you an anaesthetic it will make your mouth swell and the mould will be no good, it will be useless."

There was no turning back.

I lay in the seat staring at the ceiling.

Eerily, the dentist and three assistants didn't make a peep. Silently, they put on an extra amount of this blue clinging fixation glue to my teeth, and set them in a contraption with a small handle that protruded out of my gob.

We waited for what seemed like a lifetime for the mould to set and from the back of the room a low moaning scream escaped from the depths of me.

The pain was indescribable so I won't try – but the shock was even worse.

Meanwhile, my two dear friends nervously waited for me in the ever filling up waiting room, all sitting in line.

Shaun later made me laugh when he said they heard my woeful screams and said: "What is that Margi Clarke like? Thought she was tough – she's not like James Cagney."

They didn't realise that I never had a single anaesthetic. I left the dentist in tears with a scarf around me – I looked like a bank robber.

It took me a long time to come to terms with a tragedy of my own making. All those years in showbiz where I was paid for my gob... two pence an eyelash... a penny a freckle... all in ruins.

The face scaffold had gone.

The money spent.

It was a time when I had to go deep inside myself and activate my atomic supply to generate the healing energies, and start the long and winding road to recovery.

Taking cocaine was a crazy thing to have done, especially at that time in my life. I'd turned 40 and that's the wrong time to go and get an addiction, and then to try and release yourself from it. It delivered me to the shores of the menopause with an awful addiction.

The menopause on its own is a difficult enough dance to do, and to give yourself that burden on top – your system is totally battered and it's mind, body and soul that you've affected, especially your mental state. That's the thing about cocaine – you take it for what it DOESN'T do. It does exactly the same thing as speed, in terms of the euphoric, 'all systems go feeling' – but it's more refined.

Another regret I have from that time was missing out on a big TV role. I was put up for a part in the Granada TV series Band of Gold in 1995, only I was too ill on cocaine to attend the audition.

It starred Geraldine James, Cathy Tyson, Barbara Dickson and Samantha Morton, and was written by Kay Mellor. It was about a group of women who lived and worked in Bradford's red-light area.

It went on to be a big success and ran for three series until 1997. But I wasn't in it. Our Frank really roasted me over that because he was my agent then. And I really was too ill to go for it.

This is a letter I never got to write to me mam. A note I wish I could send now, but she knows she is in this book along with all the people I love...

I am writing to you, Man, to tell you how I messed up bad. Forgive me for reacting to your death in the worst possible way. I became the addict to something that you did your best to prevent. Cocaine – the painkiller...

I lived my life to the full when you were here, Man.

I didn't realise just how much you protected me, mainly from myself and my 'crackpot ideas', nipping them in the bud.

Well the 'crackpot idea' was a major problem – night and day Man, alone I sat chopping out lines of 'white worm'.

At one point I couldn't even leave the house, answer the phone, or face the world.

I know it wasn't supposed to be this way, Man.

I promised you I would be strong and be there for you at the end.

I guessed the best way to help you, that heart-breaking night you passed away, was to act the role of midwife, as you knew only so well how to give birth – ten times over.

That I'd be right at your side, encouraging and that I'd help you move through the pain like the rhythm of childbirth.

Your lovely blue eyes looked at me, proud of me.
You said:"I know you'll be strong, Margi, you're the
Blonde Fist."

But I was anything but strong.
The reverse happened, Mam.

Instead of grieving properly like the rest of the family, I
am feeling and dealing with emotional, painful grief, which
would wreck my body and send me out of my mind. Despair.
I feel like I've plumbed the depths and gone right down to
the bottom of the Mersey.

Night after night, I chopped lethal lines of cocaine, the white
worm burrowed a hole in my personality.
It's sucked out all that is good in me, Mam.
I can't go out the door.

I know you are going mad at me, Mam.
I can hear you say: "Go to the Kirkby drugs unit, girl."

The last thing you did, or the people of Kirkby, was to
insist against stiff opposition to open the Drug Dependency
Centre – for the addicts... people like me...but I can't go
there, Mam. I've got to find another way.

I love you with all my heart and soul.
I'm so proud to have been your daughter.

'I went to have
colonic irrigation.
I'd never heard of it before.

I thought it was a
Greek Island.

It's not...'

15. A Good Skin

There was a line in Brezhnev: "THINK you'd better give your face back to the second-hand shop you got it from."

I created my own range of health and beauty products, Soul Rinse, keen for people to keep the face they've got.

I thought, 'I'm getting on, aren't I? I'm not getting any younger, and I haven't had a face-lift or anything. Maybe it's time to share my voice and not my gob.' In my other life I paid a penny an eyelash and two pence a freckle.

I successfully sold my aromatherapy creams and potions at the Heritage Market, at Stanley Dock in Liverpool, and then just launched an online shop.

I came up with the idea a few years before. Soul Rinse was an answer to a prayer and just the right vehicle for a change of career.

I was exhausted after a box office-breaking run of panto in Snow White and the Seven Dwarves. I booked myself for the one and only time into a health farm – an austere affair more like Cold Comfort Farm than the 'Pampered Luxury' I was expecting.

Colonic irrigation was the house speciality – which I'd never heard of or knew nothing about. I thought it was a Greek island.

The evening before I had the colonic treatment. Making Out was on the telly – an episode where Chunky, a great character, robs a python and brings it home to me – Queenie.

The next morning I hopped onto the examination trolley and had a gown with a backside open, which exposed my arse to the world.

In marched a little fella of Mediterranean extraction who was to perform the colonic. He said his name was Muffeed as he prepared the tube for insertion. I asked him what his name meant in Arabic, and he replied: "Useful."

I was so relieved he wasn't British so it wouldn't be likely he knew who I was, when a little while later I was checking the tubes to see the waste coming out of me. He gasped.

"Oh my God, the woman with the snake."

'Fuckin' 'ell' I thought, 'what's he bringing out of me?'

Yes...that's right – he had watched the snake stealing episode of Making Out the night before.

I came away from the health farm experience feeling fantastic. I was Soul Rinsed. I knew then in 1989, that the name Soul Rinse would be kept like an ace up the old sleeve for use later – much later into the new century.

I couldn't get any more acting work. There's definitely a cut-off point if you're female. I was 53 and I think the line is 50.

Soul Rinse saved me and came to my aid.

I'd been a long time in show business and I never thought I could do anything else. I tried to teach acting, but I suppose I wanted it to be ME doing it so I didn't really enjoy that.

The turning point came when I fell ill with Candida albicans intolerance to yeast, which affects more than a third of women. I had to completely change my diet to rid myself of the symptoms, which can include exhaustion, muscle and joint ache, skin rashes and infections.

Yeast, I discovered, is in so many products – besides being in bread, it's in wine; it's the bubbles that make Champagne, anything that ferments.

It is really powerful.

If you are unwell, it's your duty to find out everything that there is to know about that condition.

One day I was looking in Reid's, a local bookshop, when I noticed a title called The Golden System which, at first, I thought was a book about some obscure sexual practice. But it turned out to be a book on urine therapy.

In the back of it was an advert for a Natro-Patonic College in Manchester – my old stomping ground. I wanted to train as a naturopath and found myself short of the £3,000 course fee.

That was where Gazza – Paul Gascoigne – the footballer came in. I first met him on the film School for Seduction in 2004 when he approached Angela, my sister, because he was keen to say 'hello' – but too shy to come over himself.

When I walked over to him, I thought: 'Just be gentle, Margi, don't frighten the poor lad.'

He was looking off into the distance, he was really too shy to meet me.

We did, however, become good friends. When he was in rehab, he was texting me. I was talking to him on the phone one day and explaining that I wanted to go to college but couldn't afford the fee, and he sent me a cheque the next day.

I hope that generosity's a boomerang and it comes back to him.

So I was determined to learn more about health products and I studied for a Diploma in Naturopathy at Manchester University.

I developed a muscle rub and it's really effective against rheumatism, arthritis, colds in the body...I've got a great cream for eczema. You find if you go to the chemist you get steroid-based creams and they can damage the skin, making it go thin.

That matters, because if your skin goes thin you lose your waterproofness and then you absorb more bacteria. What I'm selling is made from marigolds, which drink in electro-magnetic energy from the sun and that's what heals skin tissue. They're really gentle creams that are very effective.

I also did a 'Kop Off' cream. I just thought that Liverpool's full of love and it's blended for seduction with ylang ylang, which is a male tonic, and geranium, which is a female tonic. I'm working on the theory that if you put those two oils in a pot of cream, they cop off and you follow suit.

All the products are from natural ingredients.

My 'star product' is Spirulina, a supplement of blue-green algae super food that contains 250 nutrients.

It is the oldest food on the planet and the easiest to digest. If you take it first thing in the morning it gives you a boost of energy, and it helps with your stamina throughout the day. It boosts your immune system and it burns cholesterol. It's really good for your stomach and it's very effective against irritable bowel syndrome, acid reflux, Candida albicans, and ulcers.

I enjoy my off-screen work – it's very fulfilling.

I don't go looking any more and I'm not going to waste any of my precious time waiting for the phone to ring.

I learned that you can get job satisfaction out of all kinds of different professions.

Show business isn't the be all and end all.

I've had a fantastic time with it, don't get me wrong, I've won awards and I'm proud and delighted with the work I've done, but if the circus pulls out of town and you're not in it, you've got to get over it.

'I wake up in a hotel in Newcastle at half five in the morning and I can't find my teeth. Room service must have taken them...'

16. Back to School

I was living on Greenbank Road and it had been really quiet work wise when suddenly, out of the blue, I got a call from an agent saying that a director, Sue Heal, from Ipso Facto, a production company based up in Newcastle, wanted to come and see me about a film part.

They were coming to my house – which was a first – usually I would be the one travelling to meet them.

I made sure everything was spick and span. I painted dabs of gold everywhere - I was on one of those interior decorating numbers, where everything had to be gold.

I met Sue and her husband, Steve, and I got on with them. I gave them such a warm welcome and made sure that everything was nice when they came. They did a screen test with me in my back kitchen.

The part I was up for was in a mainstream film called School For Seduction. The plot was about an Italian temptress, played by Kelly Brook, who comes to a college with a difference called the School For Seduction Academy, teaching how to react and be part of romance.

My character was called Irene amd originally it was written for a Newcastle actress, but Sue said that she'd seen my work and she really thought that I'd bring something to it.

The film had a strong Geordie cast. It was an interesting job and I was delighted and excited to be involved. What added to it for me was the fact that I was going up to Newcastle, because it's a great city.

I'd been up there before doing promotions for Letter to Brezhnev. On that occasion, I missed the train and I had to go in my car. I remember that it was in November and it was bitterly cold. The passenger side window had been smashed, and I thought, 'I can't drive all the way to Newcastle with no window, I'll be freezing.'

So I knocked on my ex-husband Billy's door, and asked: "Billy, have you got such a thing as a window for that car?"

He went downstairs to his cellar, and came back up 20 minutes later with a piece of perspex that he managed to shape to fit the window. He gaffer-taped it on, and it ended up staying there for 18 months!

Off I went up to Newcastle. They put me in a great hotel right next to the River Tyne, which was fine by me. You know what we're like us Northerners – we like our rivers. I always think every river's like the Mersey but I got a shock when I got up to see the Tyne from my hotel room. It's tiny. You could see people walking on the bank on the other side.

I still really got to like it though, because they're different on the other side of the country, and it was a nice change for me. Newcastle's tucked away in a little cleft. On the east coast they get fantastic morning light, so there was that reverse feeling from the sunsets we're used to in Liverpool where everything comes to life late in the day. The Geordies get it the other way around.

I also think that Newcastle is a beautiful, very feminine city. You'd be hard-pushed to hurt yourself on a corner – all their buildings are bevelled in the old part of the town. And they've got bridges galore.

The people are great, too. They are dead positive the Geordies, just like us, and you can't help but fall in with them straight away.

In School For Seduction, I was playing a great character. It was an older mother/sister-type role. Irene was someone who's already been battered by life's experiences but is still in there, giving the best advice. And she has the most emotional scenes – that's where the impact happens in the movie. My screen husband was played by Tim Healy, and in the film he leaves me. I'm really shocked and distraught because we'd been together donkey's years and we'd got kids. It's that classic story – when they have a fight, he's pointing out all the photographs she's got all over the walls of her family, and he doesn't feature there.

Tim, of course, is probably most famous for his role as Geordie brickie Dennis Patterson in Auf Wiedersehen Pet, although he has appeared in plenty of other things, too.

He was fabulous to work with – he came across as someone who has never lost his roots.

We had that natural connection. I'd met him before in Groucho's, London's Soho celebrity haunt, one night. There was a big gang of us in there all around the table – artist Damien Hirst, me old mucker from Making Out, Keith Allen (who ensured I got membership as my seconder) and Tim.

That was the first time I'd met him and now I had the opportunity to work with him as an actor. I'd always admired him. I hadn't met his wife Denise Welch as such – I didn't have scenes with her in Coronation Street.

I knew her, but I didn't know her well. We had gabs, and it's easy to get on with Denise. She's another one who likes a ciggy, and a drink. Good luck to her.

I really got on with the star, Kelly Brook, too. Always in the gossip columns and with boobs to rival my old mate Alexandra Pigg.

Kelly was lovely to my daughter Rowan and gave her a collection of her old Barbie dolls.

They never asked me to change my voice for the film. They wanted me how I naturally sounded but Kelly was getting Geordie lessons off the voice coach, and she gave it a good go.

She was easy to get on with – one of those old-fashioned glamour girls who looks like she's just stepped out from a glamour magazine of the 1940s. She naturally picked up on one little tip I gave her.

Kelly was standing in a doorframe and she wasn't central to it. I said:

"Centre yourself up." I would never try and do the director's job, but I love actors and I've got a natural empathy for them.

You get surprised as an actor by various aspects of character that come out of you – I don't recognise myself sometimes when I look back at some of these roles that I've played.

I'm not into 'method acting' but I suppose if I went and studied it I'd get lots from it, but becoming the part, you're always in there with the character. I mean, it's not the character that's suddenly aware that they're not in the key light, or that it's their cue. That's YOU as the actor.

I wasn't the lead role in School For Seduction – more in support. I suppose in Brezhnev it was a 'shared lead', but I've only ever carried the lead role in one film and that was Blonde Fist.

I'm not that attracted to doing that in any case. I love being a team member, because I come from a big family and I'm used to that. I don't get upset by the politics that goes on – it doesn't flaw me.

That was one of the reasons why I could cope on Channel Five's reality show The Farm that same year. I didn't get freaked out, whereas the women on it would crack up if they laddered a tight or damaged a finger nail.

The Farm was a reality show with celebs working and living on a...farm. Paul Daniels, who I'd met when I was Margox and once tried to saw me in half, was with his self-assured young wife Debbie McGhee.

Stan Collymore, ex-Liverpool FC was there – and Rebecca Loos.

As for Rebecca, I thought: 'Isn't it amazing what these posh girls will do', as I saw her masturbate a pig.

The headlines the next day said it all. One bonus of doing that show was that I went off to Stonehenge for a second time but, on this occasion, with our American cousin Vanilla Ice.

Getting back to School For Seduction, it was a great experience because I got on well with the director – I could throw in lines of dialogue.

I threw in a line about one man that was about to be seduced by Emily Woof's character – she's setting some bad guy up in the film, and she tells him that he can't get hard and says: "It's like squeezing a tube of toothpaste" – that was one of MY lines.

Sue Heal opened up to her actors – she'd written the script but she still opened up to suggestions. Some directors don't work that way and are very verbatim. On something like Coronation Street you can't put in an 'and', 'if' or 'but'.

And you get used to a different discipline.

What I also loved about School For Seduction was those transformation scenes. I changed from Greasy Grace from outer space to something more, a person with self worth.

I was playing the girl who worked in the chippy, and at one point, at the end of the film, I'm feeling presidential because I've passed through the 'school for seduction.' That was interesting about the film, it was teaching female skills again.

I was made up that I was working and that I was with a really strong cast. I was up there in Tyneside and I could concentrate entirely on what I was doing.

There was the odd issue along the way, though. At one point, Rowan was being looked after by my mate Sandy Hughes. She's great, she's a very maternal figure herself, but Rowan, 11 at this time, did a big Bette Davies, and was having none of it. She threw a major wobble and insisted that she had to be with me.

I thought, ok, it's going to be tough and her schooling did suffer a bit, but it was more important – emotionally – for her to be with me. I was a single parent and very kindly the director, who had children herself and recognised the position I was in, allowed me to bring Rowan up for a couple of days.

So she came up, and she was delighted with the hotel. But soon after she arrived is where the horror story begins.

Around this time, I'd had a side denture put in. Of course, I hated it, and I hadn't had it fitted in that long – the indignities of old age.

The hotel had this fabulous swimming pool and Rowan begged me to go swimming after a day's filming. I said that I didn't want to because it would mess my hair up for the following day. So she settled for me sitting and watching her swimming downstairs in the pool.

I'm sitting there and in comes this lovely lifeguard. He's only young, and we're watching Rowan doing breast-stroke laps up and down the pool. He starts chatting me up, saying: "They're nice boots."

I had these nice, tight-fitting knee-high boots on. I said: "Oh yeah. I've only got skinny legs", and Rowan's giving me daggers from the pool while I'm having a nice little flirt with this lad.

So we leave the pool and order room service. The room's messy – it's upside down – but I thought I'd straighten it in the morning. I had to be up for half five in the morning.

I decided, for the first time, to take the teeth out of my head where they were safe, and put them in a glass, like your granny would do. So I took them out and gave them a good scrub, and put them in a glass. Then, unbeknown to me, somehow...the glass goes on a tray outside in the hallway, for room service to take back.

So, next morning I wake up at half past five and I can't find my teeth.

I get a little bit worried, and I turn the room upside down – it looks like a bomb's gone off.

I'd only wanted to give my gums an airing.

I should have left them in my head where they were safe, but I didn't realise at all that they'd gone down to the kitchen.

Next thing the taxi arrives for me.

I thought: 'What am I going to do? I'll have to explain to the driver that I can't find my teeth!'

He immediately rang the director and the producer, and the whole set knew – everyone knew that I'd lost my teeth.

I was getting more and more upset by this. Rowan was awake trying to help me find them. Then the manager and the housekeeper appeared in the room. And then there's a knock on the door and who comes in but the young lad from the pool the night before.

I was sitting there looking like a Chinese grandma. Rowan starts asking if I could have dropped them down the toilet, and he's got his arm halfway down the bowl looking for them. When the hotel staff left the room, feeling sorry for myself, I asked my Rowan: "Why...why...why me?"

She looked up – and out of the mouths of babes – came the reply:

"Because you're Margi Clarke – that's why."

Well, by the time I got on the set I was an hour-and-half late. And when I got there, Kelly Brook was in make-up. She'd been called a bit earlier than me because she was opening the scene.

Kelly had been two hours in make-up and she'd heard the teeth story. When I turned up I asked her if she had any Chiclets – you know, chewy teeth.

Well, that finished her off. She laughed that much she cried off the two-hour make-up job. I thought I was going to have to give her oxygen. She was in pleats.

Warren, the producer, said: "Margi, we're really impressed with you. Any other actress would have locked themselves in the Winnibago."

The teeth never showed up again. They'd gone in the glass, on the tray, down to the kitchen and into the waste disposal unit.

So they rang up an emergency dentist and said: "Can you fit Margi up with a couple of dentures?

"Can you fit Margi up with some billy bobs?"

It was so embarrassing. I had to go on first without having them in. I had to laugh in the scene, and had to put my hand over my face. I looked like I was in a restoration comedy.

But they weren't featuring me in that bit of the scene, so it was ok.

I was needed in the scene later that afternoon so they sent this car for me, and the producer gave me £300 cash to give to this emergency dentist. I'm in the car and I'm looking at the cash thinking, 'That just seems like a terrible waste to me, to give to this dentist.'

When I went in, he was a nice man and he was fixing me up. He asked how they were proposing to pay, and I said: "They've given me this cash – but you couldn't put me on the NHS, could you?" And he said: "You're not in my area."

He gave me the teeth – I was calling them practice teeth. I looked like Hong Kong Phooey.

But it certainly broke some ice. You have all kinds of experiences when you're on a film set. It is like a big family on set, you're all thrown together in unusual circumstances.

Rowan came with me to the premiere of School For Seduction in Newcastle, and it was the first nightclub she'd ever been to.

It was a star-studded event, and there was Paul Gascoigne. He was like a little atomic bomb – the lights that were coming off him. He was radiant. And I knew he was shy, but I'm attracted to shy people.

I went over to him. He was moving from one foot to the other, nervously, and I said: "Hey Paul, are you looking for a ball to head? Here y'ar lad."

We talked about his time in Liverpool, when he played for Everton, and how he had a real soft spot for the town.

We exchanged phone numbers, and that was that. Afterwards we kept in touch and he helped me out, but then he was poorly, and he went into The Priory.

'Hey Ma, if only you could
see me now. I've made it into
the big one,
Coronation Street.
I wanted to be the new
Elsie Tanner'

17. Streetwise

As a trained Granada telly presenter, it was dead weird to go back and work with them 20 years on. But appearing in Coronation Street seemed as natural as 'destiny calling'.

At this time, our Frank was acting as my agent at his Liverpool theatrical agency – Orion Production. One fine day he picked up the phone and called the executive producer of Coronation Street, Brian Park – aka the Axeman.

Frank, a very effective negotiator, got Axeman to agree to interview me for a part in Corrie. Back up to Manchester ('Mannie'), I went dolled up in short skirt and tight jumper. My blonde hair was freshly bleached, and with an extra slash of bright, red lippy applied.

I was full on – atomic supply activated. I perched myself on the corner of the very expensive table and pitched to make me the next Elsie Tanner.

I was made up to land the role of cellmate to Deirdre Rachid nee Barlow. I felt like the Bride of Frankenstein having 50,000 volts going through to my heart. The canny jailbird Jackie Dobbs was like Ronnie Barker in Porridge – Fletch to Anne Kirkbride's Godber.

Jackie was in for A.B.H. – Actual Bodily Harm – serving time for a violent attack on a woman who nicked her man. So she was now showing Deirdre the ropes about life in jail. Yet it was Anne who was showing me the ropes.

She was so kind. I dried up once and she was straight in there. She was brilliant. She said I was a 'rum do'.

I loved Bill Roache too – who, of course, plays Ken Barlow. Bill knew me from back in the seventies. I got on really well with his son, Linus, who used to come into my Margox dressing room in 1978 and sit and jangle in there.

He was totally unsnobby, Linus.

So is Bill, in the sense that he bothers to speak to people, to go and make the effort. Back in 1994, I'd been campaigning with my mother for the Labour candidate in Bootle, and Bill Roache was there campaigning for the Tory candidate. I'm on the megaphone – "Don't vote for him!" And Ken was on the other megaphone – it was like a scene from Star Wars.

When I was going into Corrie, I was a bit nervous, wondering what he was going to think. But then you get respect because he knows that I'm passionate about my beliefs, and I know that he's passionate about his. It's like the lion and the lamb lying down together.

We were sitting down chatting, and he was welcoming me to the show and that, and I asked him about reincarnation. Bill's got a druid background, and that's what interested me. And none of us are an island, my mother taught me that too, you have to try and get on with everyone.

So he's telling me about reincarnation, and I came back home and told my dad. I said: "Hey Dad, me and Ken Barlow were having a good little talk there about reincarnation, he really believes in it."

Dad said: "I know why he believes in reincarnation, it's so then he can come back and spend all that money."

Bill had really nice manners, and he makes an effort for newcomers going in there.

Like I say, I know there's a northern rivalry between our two cities but Manchester has always been lucky for me – it's where I have been given my big breaks – from Margox to Making Out. So I won't hear a wrong word said about it.

I was proud to be in a long line of Liverpudlians to join 'The Street', which made stars of Geoffrey Hughes (Eddie Yeats), Jean Alexander (Hilda Ogden) and Kenneth Cope (Jed Stone). Bill Kenwright (Gordon Clegg) was an early lead and then decades later there was Michael Starke (Jerry Morton) and Craig Charles (Lloyd Mullaney).

I learnt to love the character of Jackie Dobbs and when I got the script and read about her character, I was delighted. I always am – I never think, 'Oh, not another stereotype'.

I'm delighted to be working, to have an income. I'd well come to terms with the fact that I would only be given certain types of roles. That's probably why I enjoy doing my music – I get variation of expression in other ways – recording and making pop videos.

And anyway, they are interesting characters to play.

Soap operas are built around female characters. By and large they are the most interesting, because the male characters tend to follow a more predictable storyline – they don't break out of the male condition that much.

The class system follows you around in show business, and calls in typecasting. You could say to someone like Joanna Lumley, "Don't you get fed up playing posh?" – it's just as valid a point.

I could see through all that. If you weren't prepared to change your accent, take a blowtorch to your past, de-louse the Scouse, then you had to accept what you got.

Alexandra Pigg did just that – she took elocution lessons. She's well content now – got lovely kids, a fabulous fella and a great house. But I knew that I'd made a contract with mission control – some people call it God – to tell the truth.

By the time I'd joined Corrie in 1998 I was already emotionally unwell and was in the throes of addiction. I was running my batteries too high, because cocaine revs you right up. It probably made the character more of a blast than I would have wanted. If I'd have approached it now I would do it differently, but I didn't seize the opportunity.

That was a terrible decision.

Being in Coronation Street is like being in the royal family. It's that massive and when I did those scenes with Anne Kirkbride in the jail, and I was the old lag that knows it all, it was being debated in parliament because the whole country was up in arms about poor Deirdre being in prison with me. You'd have to create mass murder to get that kind of publicity as an actress. Even the Prime Minister was gegging in on it.

Anne is a fabulous actress, really, really subtle. She was emotionally affected by what she was playing and she'd been through all that trauma of the court scene, and the way the audience received it.

That was the first time that any mainstrean soap had covered the whole of the country with a story. That was the one everyone was talking about, and I think Anne was affected by that – she'd get really, really upset. My character was trying to wise her up. I've never been in prison, so it wasn't something I could draw upon. I've had a night in a cell, but I've never been in prison and I hope I never go. But I'm from the working classes aren't I, so I know all about that.

At the time, I too was affected by the ill effects of a dangerous lifestyle.

I was lucky, again, in that I found it easy to fit in on the set, due to having worked at Granada as Margox. A lot of the other actors knew me from those days. When I went back I probably did push some noses out of joint.

While I was in the big time, I was doing lots of TV and radio interviews. I did some stuff for Pete Price. Frank knows him and Pete is gay, and like I said, I support all those who have supported me.

Pete is on Radio City. This celebrated DJ has a book out called Namedropper. He loves his soaps and knows all about the characters. So he knew all about me and Jackie Dobbs.

Going in the Rovers Return for the first time was really intimidating. You've got to gather your wits about you, because now you're playing in a scene with the whole cast. It's quite competitive in the sense that you don't want to get anything wrong. The sets are amazing places to go on – it's a massive room, like an aircraft hanger, all separated off inside into different living rooms. When you're looking at it from on the floor, you're seeing that magic box – but you're also seeing it with the cameraman on a big dolly and he's ten foot overhead in the air, with the microphone on it like a big fishing line.

What's interesting is the power of the concentration that everyone contributes. Every last person in that room is at the top of their jobs. The crew are the best in the country on every level. It's a top show – even to the supporting artistes – the best ones are on the soaps. They're the best paid of all the supporting artistes. You can feel the electricity from everyone's concentration.

If you're nervous, it comes out in different ways – your voice might go slightly higher, for example. I always feel sorry for other actors if they blow the scene. Sometimes you can have a conflicting feeling to that because you might be made up that they're blowing the scene, because you might have made a little fluff that gets through. But if someone else blows it, you get another chance to have another bite of the cherry.

Actors will look out for each other, if say you might be handling the props wrong, or they'll look out for the first-time directors. Beverley Callard was good like that. There's good camaraderie. I think in the old days it used to be like MI5 in the Green Room – you'd have to be careful what you said because it could end up in the newspapers the next day.

I was sad when I left, because I knew that I was going to be really disappointed about it further down the line.

And I knew I blew the opportunity.

They brought me back as Jackie Dobbs in 2008, but I did blow a very good chance first time around to stay in work for a long time, and have all that comes with it.

Before I left, I threw in a last line of my own, when I was put in that taxi heading off the Street for the final time.

I said: "See ya', don't wanna be ya'," and they left it in because they knew it was great for the character. When I got a call from the stand-in executive producer, it was a sign that they weren't keeping me on.

Apparently, they always praise you before they sack you, but I'd never been sacked off anything before so I didn't realise that was what they did. It's not like a normal sacking, but that's what it is, they were not renewing my contract.

I was walking the plank, that's how it felt.

First of all, he was telling me how marvellous I was. I'd never been a prima donna on set – it's not my style – I'd rather get set against the grindstone, and play ensemble. But I was being a little bit outrageous.

My personal life – my relationship – wasn't going well, which landed me on a tabloid front page, and I wasn't paying enough attention to the job.

It was still a shock when they said it was game over, because I didn't see it coming. I don't really know the full story as to why they made that decision.

You could factor in all sorts of things – Jackie was never going to be in there permanently, I had a strong Liverpool accent in a Manchester show that was identified by its accent, and I was flying close to the wind – they might have picked up on the grapevine that I was using cocaine. So I think there were many factors – but you never get to know.

I was in Corrie the first time for about eight months, and then there was another six-month period. Then with a new pink hairstyle I returned in 2008 to cause more trouble. There were more lives to ruin.

I made my way to Lime Street on the 82 bus at least an hour early for my interview with the producer, Kim Young, in Manchester.

I sat upstairs at the back of the bus on a beautiful May afternoon. Looking outwards to the west across the River Mersey, at the rolling hills of Wales 30 miles off in the distance, the clear blue sky promised to hold out for the rest of the day – maybe Manchester would be cast in the same western optimism.

So much had changed in my life since I was last in the Street, nine years before. My chronic lateness had finally been overcome as I went past every single station platform that trundled the straight line from west to east along the same track as Stevenson's Rocket.

My walk from Oxford Road station took me to a Manchester I hardly recognised. Just like my hometown, the interior of the great northern concubine had been turned inside out like a sock.

The new Urban Splash development squeezed down the Georgian backstreets to the mecca of celebrity – Granada Television Studios.

When I first got the phone call saying I was back in, I stood in my kitchen and cried tears of joy.

And then I spoke to my mam.

She was a Corrie fan and I was still grieving for her when I first appeared on the show first time around.

I believe that what you see with Jackie Dobbs isn't what you get with me. I am a harmoniser – who plays aggressive roles!

But I don't like aggression myself unless it's beautiful in spirit.

Everyone thinks I'm like the characters I play, but I'm not. There's an aspect of me that can throw a punch, but I love people.

Acting is just playing and it's a privilege to play – it's like being a kid again.

"'Mom! Mom! There's a **millionaire** giving money away on the beach!" I didn't realise he was talking **about me** and I asked: "Where, kid?"'

18. Reality Bites

Anne Robinson once tapped me on the shoulder in a post office and said: "We've never met – but my mother loves you."

Now I remembered Anne from What The Papers Say, years back.

I used to watch her with my mother but she was a bit to the right of us politically.

So, when she said her mother 'loved me' I asked her why, and she said: "Because she was a chicken stuffer."

I brought my fist down to her and said: "See that arm? I've done two thousand chickens' arses a day with that."

And she burst out laughing.

That was the little gab that we had in that post office.

I'd never seen her since that encounter, until I got the chance to go on her famous programme – The Weakest Link.

It was actually 'Celebrity Strong Women Weakest Link' and I did it in 2006. I was on there with eight other formidable females including comedienne Jenny Eclair, broadcaster Jenni Murray and PR guru Lynne Franks. I finished fourth, which wasn't too bad, and I had the usual bit of banter with Anne. I gave as good as I got.

In the later stages of my career, different opportunities have come along to get involved in various TV programmes.

Cash in the Attic, the BBC daytime show that hopes to uncover people's hidden treasures at home and then sell them at auction for charity, was another one I was invited on.

I was filmed with my Rowan as Angela Rippon and the Cash in the Celebrity Attic team came to Liverpool one beautiful, sunny day, and then my items went under the hammer at Cato Crane auctioneers in Stanhope Street, Toxteth.

I had to trudge down memory lane trying to retrieve bits of treasure from my life. Most of the items came out of my dad's attic in Kirkby.

Me and my sisters took a ladder to the loft and came out with stuff we had totally forgotten about. I found an old jewellery box from the '70s that my mum had bought from TJ Hughes. The items are sentimentally priceless to me, because they belonged to my family and evoked so many memories.

I gave two photographs, one of John Lennon and one of George Harrison that were on my mantelpiece and all the proceeds went to Greenpeace, which was my chosen charity. I even had a go at being an auctioneer.

"That's yer lot..." I said when I smacked the gavel down.

Then – from the sublime to the ridiculous – I also signed up for Celebrity Total Wipeout.

I am naturally still quite fit – running everywhere. So I signed up to do it – with people I'd never heard of because I don't watch telly at all. I'm a snob – I've always got me nose in a book instead. I just like being on it.

It was filmed in Venezuela, which was a country that surprised me. I'd heard tales from my grandad, who would talk about it. Yet when I got there it seemed so new. I loved the people. Families there had, like, ten kids each. It reminded me of Liverpool.

Before I did the various energetic tasks that the physical show demands, I'd been in the catering room where they'd laid on a lavish spread for the contestants. I was hungry and stuffed my self with anything and everything.

Then I did all the gruelling events.

I'd be running up to the famous red balls and then I fell in the water which was 20 foot deep.

Well...

After all that and drying out I wasn't feeling the best. I was thinking that maybe all that food beforehand wasn't such a good idea.

Then I spewed up...a Spanish omelette. Well, you would, wouldn't yer? No one came near me after that.

I'll definitely be watching what I eat before I do one of my latest charity stunts. I always wanted to say a big thank you to my 'second home' Manny – Manchester.

So, when I was invited to abseil down the Manchester Town Hall in 2010, I readily agreed. Well, I thought I'd give it a good go, my best shot – that's what I always do – no matter what I am doing otherwise, what is the point?

It was to raise money for a paraplegic charity. I agreed to it and then a day later I thought: 'Oh, no, what have I let myself in for?'

I guess that's my take on doing work like that – putting something back in. I don't ask questions, "there's only solutions," as John Lennon said. I was very happy to do that because of the much-respected newspaper about disability, run by Tom Dowling called All Together, who wanted to interview me.

I've still got ambitions. There are other shows that appeal to me. I enjoy Come Dine With Me, I'd love to appear on that and I've always watched Who Do You Think You Are as I've got a fascination with where we come from and who we are.

That leads me to another chapter in my life that you may find a bit unusual. I believe in UFOs...if you want to know why, we'll have to go back to 1995.

I was returning home on a plane after a romantic and spiritually expanding holiday visiting temples in Bali with a boyfriend – my much-loved old friend the musician Alan Gill. 'Birkenhead-the-ball', he was a 'soul sailor' and gifted spiritual trainer.

As an exercise in letting go we freely gave away £1600 pounds to the poor locals on the Indonesia beach.

At one point, with crowds of happy people around us sharing my wages it became hot and thirsty work.

While I collected drinks from the hotel bar, I left Alan dole-ing out the dough on the shore. As I was making my way back with two fruit-juices in hand, a freckle-faced American boy came running in the bar puffing and panting.

"Mom! Mom! There's a millionaire giving money away on the beach!"

I didn't realise he was talking about ME and I asked: "Where, kid?"

I have to say it was one of the most freeing and liberating gestures I'd ever done, and rewarded me with a strong loving connection to humanity.

The realm where my artistic muse went returning the answers and solutions I was now aware of began to inform my life.

The spiritual climax came at the end of the holiday and returning on a homebound plane to England.

We took our seats near the front and after our friends the trolley dollies cleared away the half-eaten plastic food, chilled out Alan, who could take the 'knock' anywhere, fell fast asleep.

Sitting beside Alan, I was feeling full of love. Content and happy. I had nervously told him earlier that day that I might be pregnant. I was over two weeks late with a period. I was about 41 years old at the time – so it must have been my last 'dinosaur egg'.

Alan was as delighted as me at the possibility of the growing pregnancy and chinked a glass of bubbly in the hope of what might come of it. Then he fell asleep.

An hour later and feeling restless I decided to go for a wander. I walked down the tightly-seated aisle, where most of the passengers were asleep like Alan.

I took up a standing position at the very back of the plane and looked out at the night sky through the rear-view window.

Now you see me ...

At the Liverpool
Empire 1995, in panto

... now you don't

Giving it some lippy as
the Wicked Witch

What's it all a pout,
Margi?

A cheeky promo shot for Carlton's
The Good Sex Guide, in 1994

Broken Angel

A promotional shot for I Hired a Contract Killer, in 1991, reflecting on where my next job would come from ... on a wing and a prayer

Viva Vivienne –

She does it for me, from head to toe.
Pure Westwood

Noshin' a carrot promoting my best-selling Better Than Sex Cookbook in 1996

Raw Woman Power!

But, I wish I'd washed my feet before the photo shoot

Explosive ingredients
- Love and Lust

I'm mixing a love
bomb for Britain
in The Good Sex
Guide, in 1991

The Good Sex
Guide turned on
13 million viewers ...
myself included!

I've always played a brassy, hard-nosed blonde but Ian McShane was the first to turn me soft. I played Connie, his love interest in the 1995 mini-series Soul Survivors. The accent was on playing a quieter me

Relatively speaking ...

Family Affairs in 2001 (left). I played David Easter's mum, even though I was only five years older than him! He actually had more grey hairs than me

Hold on, girl ...

A confrontation scene from an episode of this popular soap, filmed in Teddington, London. I'm good at doing them

I'm NOT the Weakest Link

I enjoyed some real banter with Anne Robinson in 2006 during a celebrity 'all women' special of the long-running BBC quiz show

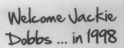

Welcome Jackie Dobbs ... in 1998

Cheers to me man Frances, who sadly never got to see me in the Big One – Coronation Street

One of my many roles on stage. This is a version of Night Collar where I played a prozzy. Why do I keep getting cast as a prostitute?

Getting funky with Chunky (played by Brian Hibbard, better known as a member of the Flying Pickets pop group). We were Spanish dancing in an episode of Making Out – 1989

A lovely mumsy shot of me and my beautiful baby girl, Rowan. I took her on the set of The Good Sex Guide and fed her between scenes

Double Act

My, how she's grown. I hope Rowan follows in her musical mum's footsteps

With my lovely brother Frank, without whom none of it would have been possible. We are pictured in 2010 after supporting Clapperboard UK – (Maureen Sinclair's inspirational organisation helping young film makers of tomorrow). Frank's on the left...

Late night chat show queen.
Gabbing me gob off and making
wavelengths at City Talk

Loose cannon!

Me in 2010 when I was made Queen
of the Seas for the International
Pirate Muster in Liverpool

I found myself looking directly at two separate and gorgeous pink lights, just a short distance from the tail fin of the plane.

I was so transfixed and I remember a complete calm coming over me. Deeply relaxed and on the beta waves, I calmly took in the two pink lights with spiral vortexes in the middle. A moment later I was joined by a tall, blonde handsome man about 32-years-old, clean-cut with a Nordic appearance.

He too looked out the window towards these spinning lights, just about 100 yards from the plane and told me in a direct but peaceful manner:

"They have been following the plane since Moscow."

I wasn't shocked or even startled, just incredibly relaxed even though I had never seen a UFO before or anything so captivating or strange as the two pink lights.

The 'Norski Angel' standing beside me broke my gaze again and asked:

"Are you travelling alone?"

For the first time in the encounter I felt a wave of anxiety surface and, looking the spotless man in the face, I firmly told him:

"No, I'm with my boyfriend."

I registered another little shock wave as my penetrating stare for a nanosecond saw the binary coded computer in his eyes.

By now beginning to feel tired, I decided to sit in the empty single seat reserved for the airhostess. I don't know why I just didn't return and take my seat at the front next to Alan.

Within a few seconds I was asleep, dreaming dreams I couldn't recall – then woke up about 20 minutes later.

Once again I looked out the windows and, yes, the pink lights were still there.

And then, sadly for me, I felt the warm monthly flow...

I became a UFO enthusiast from that moment on and love to read and watch the massively informing material on the Internet

I've recently read about the ongoing mystery surrounding a tiny object that orbits Mars (approximately 27 miles across and 7 miles long). Why, in the whole of the Solar System is the only 'moon' that is not spherical and round like it should be a unique potato-shaped nugget?

Speculation has mounted from previous probe pictures that suggest that the 'Luna nugget' is an Ancient Spaceship. I do think sometime very soon human beings will take their rightful place in the cosmos as we are introduced at last to the 'neighbours', finding cosmic company.

In my view, the universe is teeming with life and I sometimes wonder if there's a child in space – the image of Alan and me.

I know people will think I am nuts. But it's my truth. It's my view on the universe. I always try and tell the truth – that is what emerged from the punk era – it was truthful and honest and open.

I would love to present a TV documentary about the subject called 'Finding Cosmic Company: Margi Clarke's Guide to Our Friends Upstairs'. And I would love, one day, to be able to afford a huge tele-scope to look up there – from my south Liverpool home.

The interest in life elsewhere gave me an idea for a song recently. I've always made music, and recorded with a lot of different artists. It's another ambition of mine to represent the UK in the Eurovision Song Contest.

I enjoyed my first attempt at getting there in 2010 with my song Holographic Disco, recorded in the home of my friend Steve Jones.

We did the whole thing in Steve's back kitchen in a house not far from where John Lennon used to live.

He and Dennis Murphy are great with the technical side of things, so they put together a video after I recorded it in front of a green screen on the tiniest piece of stage imaginable.

Then they super-imposed me performing at Glastonbury.

I wrote the lyrics, which relate to my interest in UFOs, outer space and 'exopolitics' – the study of extraterrestrials and their contact with Earth's West Coast governments.

The video went out on You Tube and I did an electro-dance style. This was yet another side of me. This time I was a 'leccy electric' pop star. Mind you, I am old enough to be Lady Gaga's granny.

'An individual is only as strong as where he or she comes from. John Lennon told the truth and I loved the way he never stopped trying to tell it'

19. Liver Bird

The women of Liverpool are beautiful and the men have handsome faces. I can tell our faces straight away – they've all got open gobs, nice skin and great complexions. It stuns people when they come here because they can't believe there are so many belles of the ball.

I was on the Terry Wogan Show years ago and saying the only thing that's common about my home city is the beauty of its people – but WE take it all for granted. We are different because Scousers STILL own their city. We can still make our voices heard and we can still tell our stories.

Liverpool is a good example of what my mother used to say to me: "An individual is only as strong as the group he or she comes from."

My birthplace is full of big families, unions and communities – and yet, we have got loads of mad, crazy individuals too, and that twain ain't supposed to meet.

Me mam was the archetypal northern matriarch and she, and my late dad, Mick, were great singers and performers who loved their community. I know I harp back to it but it's true – and stays with you...it will always stay with me.

We used to joke that mum's second name was 'Reduced' because she loved a bargain.

I was privileged to be brought up by two such fantastic, working-class parents.

I had such an active upbringing because me mam took me on that many demos. We also learned that if you demonstrated against something you could get results.

I've got so many homegrown heroes – like Crissy Rock, who's a brilliant actress because she gets right in the moment. As well as her acting, she does a nightly stand-up show in Benidorm – she works really hard.

John Lennon is another hero and our city will never forget him. I loved the way he tried to tell the truth – and told it. He was a genius.

Henry Epstein, nephew of Brian Epstein, is an incredible man who's still keeping the flame burning. He's been involved with loads of bands. Then there's my daughter, Rowan, who loves her music and my son, Laurence, who co-runs Bad Format, a classic Liverpool cellar bar and venue in the city centre.

I love the professionalism of the actor, writer, comedian and DJ Neil Fitzmaurice. Neil, who co-wrote Phoenix Nights, can tailor his act to suit different audiences. I've seen him perform material in front of kids and then to all age groups – he's excellent. He's also a really good actor.

As for Kirkby...it's beautiful.

I love St Chad's Church – my mum and dad are buried there. I love Kirkby people – they would do anything for you. Far more people with life-threatening illnesses are nursed at home in Kirkby than anywhere else in the country.

I also love St Helens people, too – they really look up to Scousers because we're like their older brothers and sisters. I love their innocence and tell them: "You're not woolybacks, you're fluffies!"

As for the River Mersey...like the Clyde, Tyne and the Thames – everything starts with the river, which is the life force and heartbeat of the city, pumping energy that comes from our city, at the banks at Birkenhead over to Liverpool itself.

We shouldn't ask "What time is it?" but "What tide is it?" That's a line from a great book called Edgy Cities.

We used to have the bus station there – it was Destination Pier Head, and to lose that was a big wrench. There was even a recording booth where you could cut your own record.

I sometimes think about classic Liverpool characters who sold the Liverpool Echo, like Woxy and Sandy.

Walking around the city stimulates your appetite and I like to go to Maggie May's café in Bold Street for some great Scouse, run by a really great family – led by John Lea, who has a travelling Scouse van. (Sort of like an ice-cream van, but filled with our traditional dishes of Scouse, peawack soup and wet nellies.)

I love sitting in the window of that café and watching the world and his wife go up and down Bold Street.

Bold Street was Liverpool's Bond Street.

I always take people down Mathew Street, just to let them have the 'feel' of music that's been perpetual in Liverpool since before The Beatles. Liverpool families love singing – we love being vocal and being heard.

Another place I like is Williamson Square, where you can also watch so many people go by. It's great to see how nice people are to each other and will start up conversations and tell you their life stories. I've told loads of people my business on the back of a bus...I'm always on the number 82.

Liverpool bus drivers are the best in the country, in my opinion, and I've worked everywhere – they always wait for you if you are legging it to catch the bus.

I think buses are great because I love the fact that fellow commuters will likely join in. They are dead confident but, sometimes, they don't realise how confident they really are. Others sometimes misread that confidence as arrogance – but it's about the joy of life and wanting to make the most of it.

I like the 'old' museum in William Brown Street – it holds dear memories for me of coming down on the bus on Sunday afternoons. It's still a great place for kids to go.

I mourn the old Quiggins store – that was great and somewhere alternative where kids could hang out. I know there's a new version, but I don't like the building – it looks like Gaudi on acid or a bad trip on a ghost train.

I don't mind Liverpool ONE but what I am offended by is a big black coffin (a new apartment block) at the Pier Head. It's an insult. Will Alsop's Fourth Grace, which would have been so good for the city, was knocked back but, somehow, this architectural casket has been allowed to be slapped down. I was in shock when I first saw it.

I love St John's Beacon. The lift takes three minutes to reach the top of the 'Penis in the Sky'. It's not a bad place to come to work and I got the chance to do just that when I enjoyed a stint as a DJ for one of our local radio stations.

The slim, 500ft concrete column is home to Radio City and City Talk.

The glass outer shell gave out awesome panoramic views stretching out to Blackpool 50 or so miles away. But what thrilled me the most was the pounding power of the Mersey, and each night before the show, I got off on the liquid-green crystal waters.

I would take all that in and get energised for a good gabbin'. A three hour 'chew' with the listeners, because now I was a broadcaster for real. My own all-talk gab fest.

This time it echoed back to the TV series Soul Survivors in 1995 with Ian McShane. That film was mentioned earlier in the book and was set in a radio station in St John's Beacon 13 years before.

It called back to me and I thought back to that small hub-like studio in drama and now here I was in the real thing, ready to broadcast to an appreciative audience.

The listeners reflected the local area – guests and incoming artists who shared their projects and causes with me while I took calls to our resident astrologer Gaynor – the best psychic in town.

I loved the 'switched on feel' of the mic when the gab got goin'. And the very first call of the Saturday show at 10pm would be my dad – 'Iron

Mick' – who would take us on an amazing journey down memory lane back to the hard, but happy life they had in the 1930s and the Second World War.

My dad would finish up with one of his many songs, maybe Cole Porter, Irvin Berlin or Jimmy Rogers.

'Iron Mick' had a brilliant voice and he surrounded us as a family with song. He sang like a lark throughout his life.

He was a big hit with the listeners, who then consoled me at his passing six months after we started broadcasting.

I'm so glad about my dad's shows – those he did with me – they were a fitting tribute to a great raconteur.

A year later the gabbin' stopped...City Talk's schedules were revamped – a victim to the recession. I was no longer on air.

I enjoyed being an agony aunt, though, promoter of the arts, giving the mic out to people.

I always stood up when I did my show   I never sat down. I was the best stand-up chat show host in the country – for a while.

Of course, I still live in Liverpool.

I don't live far from Lark Lane in the south of the city and I love it there – it's a brilliantly-mixed area; there's loads of us, loads of locals and plenty of out-of-towners and career people.

It's a laugh, it's not expensive and it's got that Liverpool village feel to it – and it's right next to Sefton Park, which is a great place to feed ducks...I love to feed ducks.

'I never have

or never will go

anywhere

without me bits ...

even when

I'm 70'

20. 2025

At the turn of the new century, I bought a computer. Well, you have to keep up with things, don't you?

I am completely technophobic, but I was still able to launch myself into cyber-space via AOL.

I made a beeline for a chat room, and billed myself as Can't Talk Won't Talk. I just wanted to watch the chat from the sidcline, but my nom de plume certainly got me a response – so many people wanted to talk to me.

I did venture in eventually and had a really good chat with someone in America. Later on I went online using my own name. That was a mistake, because I'd find myself saying things as Margi that I shouldn't. I kept expecting my remarks to appear in the papers the next day. I tend to be frank by nature, which can be a risky business.

I went back to chatting incognito. And I chatted so much that my machine got clogged up and kept grinding to a halt until I learned how to tidy and delete files. It was just fun and wonderful to make a connection with people thousands of miles away.

Computers can be called the modern door bolt, because everyone stays in to use them. And doesn't time fly in front of that screen?

I get shocked when I look at the clock and find I've been sitting there having a ball for hours on end.

There are dangers, of course. I once came across a shocking site with a horrifyingly graphic picture of someone being shot in the head. That's not something I wanted in my memory, but the image is there forever now. It really upset me.

I love email and I use the computer to write, and keep, letters to casting agents. I can use the same letter each time and personalise it. And I do write some short stories on the computer as well – just for my own entertainment. I'm not going to win the Booker Prize, but I can have a laugh. I think this technology encourages people to be creative.

Another fun thing I did was look up sites about me, and amazingly there were quite a few. One young lad called Barry has created a site about me with the most fantastic pictures. I barely remember them being taken. It blew my mind. I sent him an email and he was delighted that I was on his site.

He asked if he could continue to speak about me. I said: "Yes, as long as it's not detrimental stuff!" I was astonished at how much he knew about me. He had gone to so much trouble to find out about my work over the years.

On another site, a bloke talked about how he met me in a chippie in Liverpool, and lent me 50p. Another guy said he'd met me on a train and I'd given him two ciggies.

When my vegetarian cookery book came out, I went online to try to promote it. That was great – talking to 20 people at once. I liked the fact that I could be more politically adventurous than I could ever have done in a printed interview.

Things have changed on TV. In the old days, wherever you came from, whatever your colour or creed, what mattered was talent. Talent was the currency. Now it's nothing to do with talent anymore. You get famous for being on things like Big Brother. I believe the Internet will redress the balance.

The Internet produces new ways of doing business, and new ways of expressing ourselves, and also makes us more similar to one another. There is a freedom and democracy there.

I sometimes like to try and look into the future, imagine what life will be like. I wouldn't be surprised that in 2025 Liverpool was the capital of the country. Wouldn't surprise me in the slightest.

If that does happen, my hometown will occupy an even stronger position than it does now. The investment tax effect...maybe I'm not that far off the mark.

I hope by 2023 I'll be an all-round useful storyteller. I hope I can deliver gem tales, as I like to call them, of this period in time. And the juicy social stories that are important to protect the young wits, so that they've got it as well.

I could tell them all about the Mary Ellens and all of us who went without. And then you can tell them about how we improved our lot – expanded our consciousness – compared to where our grandparents were.

So I will be an old storyteller.

I love that tradition to keep the gabbing going.

I hope to be able to say: 'It's been a life worth living – definitely'.

Life's amazing isn't it...even a cold sore wants to live.

Everything wants to live.

We've been blessed with that.

I used to say to myself when I was at my lowest ebb, when I had no money – I didn't have a bean – I'd look in the mirror and say, 'well you're richer than all those poor dead fuckers'.

I'll probably be a scruffy old age pensioner. All I need would be my own floating landing stage.

I will always want to act and looking back and forward in my career, film always was and is the goal. That's the gold standard, to make it in celluloid. It's a different material and the magic is more sensitive and finer. When it all clicks in and it's all in the flow it's completetly symmetrical.

Acting on screen – it's great.

At 70, as I will be in 2025, I think my energies (what I value) will still be there. I hope I still have a good energetic force that I can generate. I'm hoping that I can keep that.

I think in every decade there's a plateau of youth so within my seventh decade – within that – there's a little island called youth. I've only got to swim to it or walk to it. That island – your muscles remember – your memory isn't just kept in your brain, it's throughout different parts of your body.

I've learned to keep the core of myself strong.

I learned that doing Blonde Fist.

I was always energetic. I didn't add any discipline to it. I wasn't an adult until I made that film.

I had to go into strict training. When you do, it sets up those muscles for the next decade.

So I set myself up for when I was 40.

Showbiz is a game.

The rest of the workforce is caught up in the terrible practices that go on in showbiz – it's all casualisation. Now everyone is like an actor– it's casual.

Acting is like a glorified hobby because we don't have a big industry – but I still love it all the same. I feel at my most peaceful when I'm acting because I'm using everything – it's all being put to use. Mind, body and soul goes into it and you get a lot of self-satisfaction from it.

As you get older, you do mellow out and do come to terms with things far more.

I don't need a cutting edge anymore – because I've done a lot of what I set out to do – achieved a lot of my goals.

So you're not desperate for it – you can take it...or leave it.

I like that side of it. I've been at peace with myself in that area – although I still scratch my head and think: 'Hell, how am I going to make a living?'

I am like one of those Dickens characters from The Pickwick Papers. I am not a spendthrift. I did get to learn lessons.

I like to control things my way.

I don't own a cash card. Not even one for the hole in the wall.

I draw out enough for the next three days – enough for my family and me and I walk back from the bank that way. I don't owe anyone a penny. Even though I ain't got a penny, I am not in debt to anybody at all.

There's something about poverty that protects your health. You can't indulge – it's like getting back to Cold Comfort Farm. You are austere and on rations and that means you are actually fitter not buying the biscuits, cakes and chocolate. You don't waste things like that. Now the inflation is on food – they know the score. We are made to think that everything's cheap – because you can buy a dress for £2 but, c'mon, you can't eat a frock.

I was once asked what I would have on my tombstone, and I thought how about:

I stayed true to myself. I didn't sell out
to my own ethics and principles

We could all go along that route – de-louse the Scouse and end up with an accent like Mollie Sugden in The Liver Birds, learn how to play that media prostitution game, hanging out at places in London, chasing stardom.

Stories about you running in the newspapers about anything...BUT your talent.

There's always a price and I was aware of that price then – I knew it was phoney and so I never went down that road.

I always wanted to get back home.

Because home is real. Your home doesn't entertain any of that nonsense.

It keeps it and YOU real.

Looking back, I would have loved to have done higher education. You might not believe it but I think I would have studied Astrophysics. I love anything to do with astrology.

Newspapers first got me into that because Patrick Walker was the FIRST star astrologer. By that I mean celebrity astrologer – a bit like the first rock poet Lord Byron.

I got that newspaper bug from childhood and I will always have it – even at 70.

So I love astrology, even though I was brought up a Catholic and part of the Church looks at it as the tricks of the devil.

I use astrology as an actress. It gives me background into characters. It still gives me a lot of support.

I could tell you where any particular character was from – and that's important for any actor.

You only ever get the front end of any story when you see the script, and you have to imagine what the person you are playing was in her past, the road of circumstances that made up this character.

It did bug me that I never went to University, though. I think I would have got a lot from it.

I was a bit like the character of the Scarecrow in the Wizard of Oz. I felt like him, I wanted a certificate for a brain.

But going into showbiz was part of that vanity.

Going back to the Wizard of Oz, I certainly wasn't like the Lion. I had courage, that was never in short supply. I was never scared. I put that down to low blood pressure...it takes me ages to get hyped up.

As for the Tin Man, we'll I've always had a heart...

Do yer know, going back to my tombstone, my epitaph would be...

She never went anywhere
without her bits

It's a line from Letter to Brezhnev.

So much got picked up from that film in feeding the modern dialogue. The whole country took it to its heart.

'Looking back …
Non, je ne
regrette rien.
That's Kirkby meets Paris lingo
for, "No, I regret nothing" –
life's too short'

Where To Now?

Final Word

When you think back, you find yourself wondering if you could or would have done anything differently.

If I found myself at heaven's gates and St Peter asked, "What would you like to change?" Well, I'd say, looking back, I would have approached motherhood differently. Because, you see, I had great ambitions for the stage, when I had the healthiest womb on the planet, and I should have been just like my mam and had 10 kids.

I wanted to take Laurence with me to Paris, but it would have been the worst experience to have imposed on him – he was only four.

So I left him with his father, Billy.

He was really stable, very down-to-earth, a great father and very moral, and he took responsibility and control. I regret that on some levels – it took me years to put that right, to put that trust back in there with me and Laurence.

I went off to Paris with Jamie. We only went for two weeks to begin with, but then we signed a record deal, and met this Hungarian refugee called Peter Ogi and got distracted.

I would love now to have a really loving relationship. I think I'm ready now – I've got so much to give someone. The thing about being on your own is that to begin with you miss being loved.

You really miss it, that connection – all that love and energy flowing between you. But what you miss more than receiving love is giving it, giving your love. So that's what I want the opportunity to do – have a deep, meaningful relationship. We're not meant to be on our own. I haven't got good form in that department – I've been known as a bit of a bolter.

If we had problems, I'd jump – give it toes.

But coming from such a big family, where there were always gangs of us, well, that left me with mono-mania – fear of being on your own. It's a trait that runs in big families, because you're so used to being surrounded by brothers and sisters, and their friends.

There was always someone in the house, so that you'd never get to hear your own thoughts.

I often look back and think that if I could go back in time I would equip myself with the knowledge that I've got now – the human understanding that our intentions are what we produce in this life. I didn't realise that your dreams can come true. I used to think it was coincidence, but now I believe that it's the concentration of your thoughts, over a long time, that brings your dreams to fruition. You draw your own destiny towards you.

When I was a kid I thought that there was no chance that I would be able to do it – with the Kirkby background, having had no strong education, with a strong Liverpool accent – I thought all these things would be hurdles that I wouldn't be able to get over. So knowing that dreams can come true – that is something I would tell myself. And the knowledge that love is the only thing that you take with you.

I've never been materialistic – I don't even own a handbag. I carry all my wealth on my person. You would think that I should have watched my cash more closely, because I made millions for others. I've stood next to people in show business who have had as much talent as my bunion, but they were millionaires three times over, and that was their talent. I used to get told off about that with my mam – she had more business acumen.

So I suppose if I could go back I would protect myself properly. But then, if I'd wanted to have been in Reno, then I would have ended up sitting here with millionaire status. But no, you can only take love with you.

Jamie Reid was the love of my life. I haven't got a love of my life now – only my kids. My daughter means the world to me – she's just turned 18 – and my best mates, Carlene and Lady Shaun.

But my children are the loves of my life.

Looking back over all the different roles I've played – I've had so many faces.

I've learned some lessons along the way and come through it.

I've survived, and life teaches you that you are what you are.

There are no disguises.

Shakespeare said that 'all the world's a stage'. Maybe that's true, but you can't put on an act when you're lookin' in the mirror. I've learned that.

The one face you must always answer to is your own.

Be honest with yourself. You can't put a mask on and fool your heart. Now You See Me...

P.S.

I'm still on castors – Suzi Quickstep, I'm always walking. I don't have a car and I've got to get around. And that's how I keep fit, and I love being fit.

I did own a BMW once, and I paid £20,000 cash – took it in my handbag – and I waltzed into the BMW place on St George Street, and I asked the lad: "Show me the best car you've got here."

I don't know makes of cars. I got a licence for work. I had no intention of learning to drive because I thought I was too scatty.

But when I got the part in Making Out, one of the conditions was that I had to learn how to drive.

I went for a week's intensive driving lessons around Barnet – I'd never been there in my life before.

I knew a fella from Kirkby who was on the run in the New Forest, but there I was.

At the time Jamie was working at the Strong Room, in London, and one of the guys who used to hang around there was a cartoonist for The Guardian called Captain Star – he was brilliant. His real name was Steven Appleby, and he made me a badge with a starry image of me on it with 'Mirror, Signal, Manoeuvre' printed on.

So it came to the test day, and I know it's a cliché but I thought, 'right, I'm slinging the mini on' and I put this really short skirt on – everyone told me to do it.

And I had the badge on. This guy who came out to give me the test looked like he'd never had sex in his life before.

What impressed him and passed me the test was my emergency stop. Someone pulled out right in front of me and I had to do an emergency stop for real.

And he said: "That's what's passed your test."

He also said I would have got full marks, but I didn't use the horn.

So I passed. It was a great, liberating thing. But I haven't had a car for six years – I can't afford it. And I've got used to it. I appreciate the enforced exercise that you get.

You still see me walking around.

Stop me and say hello. I promise, yer know, I will say "Hi yer" back.

Margi Clarke,
2010

Out Takes

I love tales of this and that, but especially those based in reality.
The following selection of stories all happened. I know, I was there...

What's Cooking

In 1993 I took part in the National Vegetarian Week promotion with the legendary John Peel.

We both sent in exotic meat-free dishes.

I think the much-missed Peelie went for Mushroom Pilau.

Mine was called 'Shirley Pop Bake in Red Wine'.

You can still download my recipe.

Straight Talking

I'm never overawed meeting people.

We're all the same, aren't we? There's not a ciggie paper between us.

So, when I bumped into Jonathan Powell, one of the most powerful men in the BBC at the time, I met him with the welcoming words: "Ello, Jonathan, how are you, love?

"Come over here while I ransack yer head."

Star Burst

I was once interviewed for Channel 4's Star Test, where you are asked questions by a faceless robot computer persona.

It was ahead of its time, honest and all about yourself. The machine asked me for the five characteristics that best summed me up.

I said: "Neurotic...clumsy, a touch like a blacksmith's hammer.

"I'm open – but passionate on the sly.

"I'm not wild. I'm tame.

"I'm shy and a little bit brash – because my manners go before me.

"Oh, and I'm wicked in bed."

Benidorm or Bust

In Benidorm I played Dorothy – somewhere over the rainbow. I was made up when I landed the part as it meant I could get a Spanish suntan – I could join up the freckles.

But when I got there, there was a monsoon. The crew met me in the street in a canoe.

The good thing was that I was kept on for an extra week, which meant extra money.

I still didn't get a tan though.

Family Affairs

I used to be at home visiting my mam and dad and be chatting with them. Then I'd get my hat and coat and be off, leaving them there in the house in Kirkby.

I'd go off to do This Morning for Granada and do an interview, and my mam would say to me dad as they watched the telly: "Look, there's our Margi on the telly – she never mentioned that."

Well, I never did.

I am a bit superstitious. I just do my job, go home and that's it.

I also recall my sister Jane once looking all over the house for one of her favourite dresses.

She couldn't find it anywhere.

Then she turned on the telly and I was wearing it... in an episode of Brookside.

Wogan

I was on the famous Terry Wogan BBC interview shows and he wanted to know why we used bad language in Letter to Brezhnev?

I sat there looking at him, and said: "If it had been Eddie Murphy, would you have had the cheek to ask him?

"Bad language doesn't put you in hospital or damage your health."

Return To Sender

The Coronation Street storyline for my character Jackie Dobbs, squatting in Curly's house, got close to the bone – too close for home.

Art mimicking life merged into reality, when one afternoon learning scripts in the green room I was summoned to the third floor of the executive producer's office – Brian Parks – to explain how a final council tax demand was addressed and sent first class to:

Margi Clarke aka Jackie Dobbs,
7 Coronation Street,
Weatherfield.

I told him: "It's a good job I'm getting off as it's harder to hit a moving target."

A Day In The Life

I was once trying to get ready the night before for an audition. And when I try to be good, that's often when things go wrong. So I was early getting ready and I banged my head on a cupboard.

I had concussion – without realising it. The next morning, when I got up for this audition, I had an ectopic pregnancy, again without knowing what was going on. I've discussed that already but I didn't tell you what else happened on that day.

I went to the job audition for a role in the film Bert Rigby You're A Fool, starring Robert Lindsay. The secretary was there in reception and

I said: "Have there been many gone in for this audition, love?"

She just pointed out all the used coffee cups. And there were loads, so that told me loads of people had gone in.

And she said: "Do you want a cup of coffee?" I said "yes", so she gave me a cup of coffee, and then I went in for the audition.

When I went through the door, there were these two old producers, you know, like the ones in the Muppets – two old duffers up in the box, Statler and Waldorf. And they said, in big American accents: "Pleased to meet you Miss Clarke." Instead of saying back, "lovely to meet you," I put my cup and saucer in his hand.

Then I came out with something from a Catholic mass, at one point...I'm saying this to these Jewish producers. I didn't know it, but as well as being in pain I must have still been suffering from concussion.

I never got the part.

I came out of the audition, which was in London, and I went to the tube at Tottenham Court Road. I'm standing there on the platform looking down the tunnel, waiting for the train to appear. Then some poor girl ran out of nowhere and threw herself in front of the train. To this day I cannot look down the tunnel when I'm waiting for a tube train.

So, on the same day that I'd had the best part of a miscarriage and been violently ill, I'd also had a really poor audition, and then witnessed a suicide...

Old Boilers in Mini Skirts

Like I say, I have a great relationship with my son Laurence now, although he has saved me on occasions in the past. Once I was in a nightclub in London in the late '90s with Jason Donovan, and I didn't know it was him and he said: "D'you want a line of Charlie?" and I said: "Ok, but don't let my son see."

I took the line and OD'd on it. I ran out of the club to be sick.

As I was vomiting, a paparazzi appeared from nowhere and said, "Thank you", clicking his camera.

My Laurence appeared out of the blue. He'd come out of the nightclub to look for his mother, and he saw what happened. He picked the pap guy up, who was only tiny, by the scruff of the neck and he lifted him off the ground. He's six foot five, my lad.

He said: "That's my mother. If you don't give me the film you've had it."

And he said to me: "Mam, you'll give him a picture, won't you?" He negotiated with the photographer to have a proper picture taken of me, not one where I was being ill.

It appeared, the next week, in a Sunday magazine. The headline was 'Old Boilers in Mini Skirts' – it had Joanna Lumley in it and Lulu – and I complained to our Laurence and said: "Hey lad, look at that –'Old Boilers?'" And he said:

"What d'you mean, Ma?

"It could have been one of you spewing up!"

Mother's Pride

By Frances Clarke

My mum Frances had her autobiography published in 1993.

It was called At The Heart of It All, detailing her tough upbringing and becoming someone who spoke up for others and became a part of the community.

This is me mam talking and I am so proud she is alive in this book, making a guest appearance in mine.

Miss yer, Mam. We all do.

Love, Margi

Margi and Frank both had theatrical ambitions and I encouraged them to attend the Elliott Clarke Theatre School and College, which gave them confidence and poise.

Margi appeared in various plays and secured a part in Granada's production What's On, where she presented some of the region's television programmes. She was about 23 then with flaming red hair and made everyone gasp with some of the statements she came out with. She told Greek singer Demis Roussos: "You look as if you've swallowed a couch."

Frank, meanwhile tried for various parts, but he was a little too self-conscious and writing – rather than acting – was his forté.

He sent scripts and ideas to all kinds of producers, and wrote several episodes for Brookside in its early years.

One way and another, Margi and Frank found their foothold in the profession. Frank finished the screenplay for Letter to Brezhnev and sent it around to see if any company was interested – no one seemed to be. He was getting despondent but, then, he found a way to put it on as a theatre play. People loved it.

My husband Mick said: "I don't like our Margi using all that bad language." But I told him: "Margi hasn't used it – it was Teresa...the person she plays.

"Did Tony Curtis' mother or father think he was the Boston Strangler because he played the role in a film?

"Our Margi's just playing a part."

After that, well, Mick looked at it in a different light.

The silence from the film and TV companies was still depressing Frank, and it was a demoralising time on Merseyside. Unemployment was raging and then the Toxteth riots erupted. Frank felt that he met a brick wall everywhere he turned.

Then FATE took a hand.

One of the Greenham Common campaigners came to Kirkby, but couldn't find anywhere to stay because she had two large dogs.

Frank's an animal lover, and as he totally admired the Greenham Cause he said that Fiona Castelton could stay at his flat. Within a week of her visit she wrote to Frank, inviting him to her house on the Isle of Man. Frank was unemployed, so his mates threw a few bob in the kitty. Margi threw a few bob in. So did I. (If this was a film then nobody would believe what happened next – but it's true). Frank was astounded when he arrived at the house. It was magnificent.

The Casteltons were wealthy: their business was Baxi Fires.

The family were interested in Letter to Brezhnev and said they would back it. Somebody else said they would put money in, and the whole thing snowballed from there. The budget started off at £50,000 but in the end the final film cost £350,000.

But that's nothing – that's only the tea bill on some of the films being made now. Things started to buzz.

Brezhnev was the first film made about Liverpool by people who knew the score. It was made on a shoestring, but people took the story to their hearts and willingly gave their time for little money. Established actors Alfred Molina and Peter Firth worked their socks off for something like a fiver a day. Margi and Alexandra Pigg also threw their souls into the film. It was a wonderful opportunity for local talent and for family and friends.

I was one of the women waving enthusiastically in a scene on the dockside. My daughter Angela was in the film, too. Angela had already appeared in Channel 4's Brookside as Damon's first girlfriend and, young as she was, was beginning to carve out her own career as an actress.

Everyone pitched in and put their all into Letter to Brezhnev. Some of the scenes were shot at my friend Rene's house, and she treated the film crew as if they were family. When they were shooting outside in Kirkby, they'd all come to our house in between takes. The place was packed. The budget couldn't run to a catering caravan, so I'd make everyone a butty or some soup. They were all welcome.

It was an incredibly heady time and it was even more exciting when the film was in the can and ready for distribution by Palace Pictures.

There was a premiere in Kirkby, and everyone turned out for a fantastic party that night.

Soon the acclaim for Letter to Brezhnev started to pour in.

Some were offended by its bad language, but I think that those people had closed their ears to the real message of the film and the vision of Liverpool it portrayed.

The BBC phoned to ask if Joan Bakewell could interview us for Newsnight. Not one of the Clarke family is camera shy. We were all excited by the thought of meeting the famous personality, and Eileen and I cleaned the house with a fine toothcomb in preparation for her arrival.

She was lovely, warm and sincere, and we gave her our usual welcome. The programme gave a real boost to the film.

Brezhnev was a huge hit locally – it was on at the Liverpool Odeon for six months and nationally it became a cult film.

Margi and Alexandra did a lot of promotional work, travelling to Canada and the States and appearing on chat shows. In January 1986, Margi and Alexandra were told they had won an award for Best Newcomers. The ceremony was to take place at the Savoy Hotel in London and Frank and Margi booked a room for me and Mick.

This was something else we never ever thought we'd do – stay at the Savoy Hotel for the weekend. It was an experience I will never forget, although I tried to walk in as if it was a natural, everyday event. In the evening, I wore a lovely black dress and Mick had his dicky bow on.

We were done up like dogs' dinners.

Margi looked fabulous.

At the reception we met all sorts of people – Jeremy Isaacs, Anthony Andrews, Jeremy Irons, Twiggy, Sally Ann Field, George Harrison and Barry Norman, whom I thanked for his reviews of Letter to Brezhnev.

The whole thing was an extraordinary experience and I loved every minute of it.

It didn't change my life – I'd still be down the shop with my trolley – although I revelled in the occasions when people realised that Frank and Margi were MY kids, and they'd come up and tell me how well they'd done.

My only sadness was that my other son and my eldest daughter weren't there to share the glory.

Michael would have charmed the birds off the trees, and Kathleen would have had a business-like influence on them.

For Frank and Margi though, Brezhnev was only the beginning.

Tree of Life

I come from a long line of sailors, stevedores and barrow women.
Our roots spread wide across Merseyside and Liverpool, out to
Wales and across the briny seas.

I was born on the banks of the Mersey.

My birthplace, at home on the top landing of a council tenement
at Sandhills, Liverpool.
Four years later we would be moving. . .
the Kirkby Hillbillies setting up home.
I was born on May 25th, 1954.

I'm proud of who I am.
Here's my family tree. . .

William Cornelius O'Dowd + Rosanne Davies (C. 1870)

Sarah Jane   Richard   John   Michael   Mary   William   Rose

Catherine O'Dowd + James Barrett

Catherine   Michael   Elizabeth   Ellen   Mary   James   Rosanne   John   Edward

Frances Barrett + Michael (Mick) Clarke

Michael   Kathleen   Marian   **Margaret (Margi)**   Francis (Frank)

Adam   Greg   Jonathan   Frances   Laurence   Rowan

James Barrett + Catherine O'Dowd (C.1870)

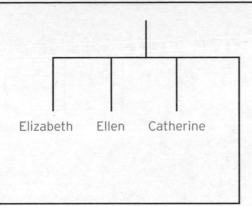

Elizabeth   Ellen   Catherine

Michael Clarke + Ann Jane McCumskey (C.1920s)

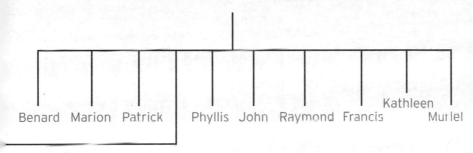

Benard   Marion   Patrick   Phyllis   John   Raymond   Francis   Kathleen   Muriel

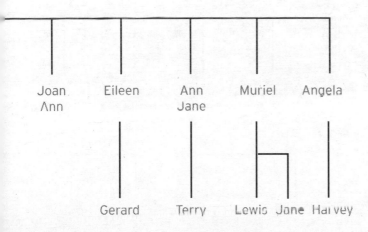

Joan   Eileen   Ann   Muriel   Angela
Ann   Jane

          Gerard   Terry   Lewis   Jane   Harvey

Margi Clarke – 'I thought, where have I gone wrong?'

Margi makes a stirring entrance

By Judith Moss

ITS fair to say that Liverpool actress Margi Clarke is proud of her city but prefers to recognise her roots.

...

Spicy

...

Gloves are off for film with plenty of punch

IT WAS a typically cosy scene of Merseyside life. Two women were squaring up to each other outside a front door when POW! one of them threw a punch which knocked the other out cold.

The husband of the assaulted woman arrived to intervene when SPLAT! he, too, was knocked to the ground.

The scene comes from the opening moments of a Merseyside-based movie Blonde Fist in which Kirkby-born Margi Clarke stars as the ...

The plot finds her progressing from champion shop-lifter and pavement scrapper to escaped jail bird and successful professional lady boxer.

Not surprisingly, Ms. Clarke admits: "I know it is going to be controversial."

So far the movie, written and directed by her brother Frank, has been seen only at the Edinburgh Film Festival and in a one-off special screening at Liverpool's new MGM cinema.

It was in the latter location that Ms. Clarke appeared in suitably pugnacious mood, where she faced a questioning audience of local film-goers.

They wondered whether its theme and language (full of the regulation effing and blinding) might give a distorted impression of Merseyside to other parts of the country.

Margi was not about to apologise for anything. The ...

... as she appears in Blonde Fist   Picture: STEPHEN SHAKESHAFT

rough language, she claimed gave the film a genuine working class flavour rather than middle class.

Besides, the rest of Britain often picked up on Liverpool's colourful language, she said pointing out that the phrase "What is she like?" now in regular use was first heard in her brother Frank's earlier movie Letter Tu Brezhnev.

As for the theme, she thought it showed women standing up for themselves.

Most of all, she was proud that the film got made at all in the middle of a recession and despite a lack of interest from the big film companies.

It was produced for a mere £800,000.

Jointly sponsored by Channel Four and British banks, the film seems to be good value.

☐ Ms Clarke with sister Angie

NO SEX PLEASE I'M MARGI'S MOTHER!

By Neal Snowdon

ZANY celebrity Margi Clarke has banned one fan from tuning in to her Good Sex Guide - her mum Fran.

Kirkby-born Margi has won awards for her frank look at the mating game.

She hasn't batted an eyelid while discussing what turns people on, advising on safe sex and testing people's knowledge of the opposite sex.

But her mum has revealed that Margi is too embarrassed to let her watch it.

Promise

Fran Clarke, an Independent Labour Knowsley councillor, has had to promise not to tune into her daughter's revealing series.

Councillor Clarke said: "Before the Good Sex Guide was screened Margi extracted a promise from me that I wouldn't watch it.

"I have always watched her in others things she has done.

"But I think Margi gets a little bit self-conscious about this because it is about sex.

"And I think she may have been a bit frightened in case I shouted at her after seeing it."

Straight talk . . . Margi doesn't mince words in her show

Margi carved a reputation as a no nonsense character in the films Blonde Fist and A Letter to Brezhnev.

Both films were written by her brother Frank, and featured music from Birkenhead-based former Teardrop Explodes guitarist Alan Gill.

Appearances in the series Making Out and late-night programme The Word also raised Margi's profile.

But her mother added: "People may be surprised to hear it after seeing her on television, but Margi is actually quite quiet.

"She is not exactly like the person she portrays."

● Eyes closed . . . Margi's mum

'I feel a bit like Maggie May's younger sister,' says Margi Clarke about her new screen role. ROY WEST reports

Margi as a lady of easy virtue in All Night Long

How the kook of Kirkby came to be a street girl in Berlin . . .

FOR a moment I imagine some erratic engineer has plumbed the phone into the drains.

Then I realise it is only Margi Clarke laughing.

...

The film's director Mike Kuetemeier (right) with cameraman Helge Weindler.

The Good Career Guide

Now You C.V. me…
Mother, stage & screen actress, pop singer,
stand-up, TV presenter,
broadcaster and now author.
Maybe I'll be a Weather Girl next

1978

The birth of Margox and the Zinc at Mathew Street, to be followed by a breakthrough at Granada Television Studios for the critcally-acclaimed and much-imitated programme What's On.

1979

Stage debut at the Everyman Theatre in Ken Campbell's Illuminatist, and a ground-breaking new play Lucky Strike, alongside Pete Postlethwaite.

1980

Paris, Polydor and the release of the single Beauty and the Thief.

1983

Tour of the North in a theatre production of Willy Russell's
Educating Rita (as Rita). Originated the role of Teresa in
Letter to Brezhnev at a modest run at the Liverpool
Playhouse.

1984

Appeared in two episodes of Channel 4 soap Brookside. Her
brother Frank wrote her in, because, as she later said, she
"had a gas bill which I couldn't pay."

1985

Letter to Brezhnev, written and produced by brother Frank,
saw Margi and Alexandra Pigg playing two Liverpool girls
who meet two Russian sailors. One of the most important
British films of all time, and inspired the whole "guerrilla"
film-making scene that eventually blossomed a decade later.
The movie was made on a tight budget, with an initial
£50,000 (one wag called this "the cocaine budget on
Rambo"). It became a huge international hit. Fans included
Michael Douglas and Beatle George Harrison.

1986

At the Evening Standard British Film Awards, Margi took the
prize for "Most Promising Newcomer". She followed this
with the European art-house trilogy for the Kaurismaki
brothers: Helsinki Napoli – All Night Long (1987), I Hired a
Contract Killer (1990) and L.A. Without a Map (1998).

1987

Makes stunning cameo in the Pet Shop Boys' video Rent.
Appears as stand-in host for Paula Yates on The Tube.

Cereal Thriller – she was also the voice for the character of "Bixie" in the Weetabix adverts. Scored a top 10 Welsh hit with Clutter from the Gutter.

1988

Appears in The Dressmaker alongside Pete Postlethwaite.

1989

Plays Queenie in the long-running (three series) of BBC's Making Out.

1990

Makes the first of her guest appearances on Channel 4's notorious music show The Word.

1991

The Good Sex Guide establishes Margi as an accomplished all-round presenter. It gained 13 million viewers – unheard of at the time for a show airing at 10.35pm. Portrayed Ronnie O'Dowd, a feisty female boxer in the Frank Clarke-penned and directed film Blonde Fist. Performed with Half Man Half Biscuit on the cover of the Edith Piaf single No Regrets (Non Je Ne Regrette Rien).

1992

Opened the Pingot Day Centre in Widnes for adults with learning difficulties. Margi still supports many charities with guest appearances.

1994

A second series of The Good Sex Guide proves equally successful with the British public, and a third series,

The Good Sex Guide Abroad, soon followed. She wins a Best Presenter prize from the Royal Television Society. Margi is offered her own daytime show, and the resulting Swank ran for two series. Stand-up and be counted – she takes a new role as stand-up comedienne. Tours her one-woman show 21st Century Scutt around the country, including a stint at the Edinburgh Festival and the Royal Festival Hall. Margi pose nude while nine months pregnant with her daughter Rowan. The resulting pictures were a 'take' on the famous Vanity Fair spread by Demi Moore. It was well received.

1995

Appears in the critically-acclaimed BBC mini-series Soul Survivors co-starring Ian McShane, Isaac Hayes and Antonio Fargas – AKA Huggy Bear.

1996

Releases Margi Clarke's Better Than Sex Cookbook, published by Hodder & Stoughton.

1998

Joined Coronation Street as jail bird Jackie Dobbs. Becomes a cult figure...again.

2001

Joined cast of Channel Five soap Family Affairs, staying for just over year. Guest stars in Casualty (the series that is, not a real hospital).

2002

Appeared in Revengers Tragedy, directed by Alex Cox and

starring Christopher Eccleston. Features in 24 Hour Party People – the biopic of the Factory/Hacienda days in Manchester, which Margi was a real-life part of in her 'Margox' alter ego of the 1970s. She also appeared as a guest on the long-running BBC show Through The Keyhole, which she said was "through the shithole." Not the programme – her house.

2003

The Boys From County Clare feature film followed, in which she played the role of Dove.

2004

Appeared in Channel Five reality show The Farm, with Rebecca Loos and Stan Collymore. She kept away from pigs. Landed a leading role in the theatrical film School For Seduction, with Kelly Brook.

2005

Opened Soul Rinse, a successful online health and beauty range which she runs parallel to her acting career.

2006/07

Margi has a role in an episode of the Hollyoaks spin-off Hollyoaks: In the City. Appears as a contestant on a celebrity version of the BBC game show The Weakest Link, hosted by fellow Scouser Anne Robinson. Margi is heard on the airwaves of 105.4 Century Radio in the north-west as a co-presenter of the breakfast show and their late night phone-in projects. Appears as a guest on Big Brother's Big Mouth on Channel 4 with Pete Burns – her close Liverpool friend.

2008

Margi is one of around a hundred local celebrities hoisted, hidden in a blue container by a crane 30 feet into the air, landing on the main stage at St George's Hall in the city. The celebrities stepped out of the container marked "Precious Cargo" to rapturous applause. On the same evening, Margi appeared as a panel guest on the BBC's Newsnight giving her take on her home town's Capital of Culture celebrations. Margi joined Liverpool's newest talk radio station City Talk 105.9, presenting a late night show on Saturday evenings from 10pm. Enjoys a prime-time role in the second series of hit British comedy Benidorm.

2009/10

Reprised her role as Jackie Dobbs in Coronation Street. Appeared with daughter Rowan in an episode of the BBC's Celebrity Cash in the Attic – and the popular Celebrity Wipe Out, filmed in South America. Appears for the first time as a granny in an episode of the BBC's Waterloo Road. Chained to railings, wearing motorbike gear shouting out at injustice...so no change there.

When a girl gets to 40 she sometimes needs a bit of a lift

By Debbie Johnson

■ It's a date that every woman dreads.
■ Once you get to the big 4-0 there's no hiding place for sags, bags and wrinkles.
■ And what better way to treat yourself on your 40th birthday, than to try and stop time in its tracks with a facelift.
■ Margi Clarke — the woman who spares no blushes with the Good Sex Guide on TV — has just clocked up 40 but refuses to let the wrinkles take over.
■ Kirkby-born Margi spent her birthday getting a Wrinkle Tone facelift from her friend Sandra Blythe, who runs Blythe's Hair Studio on Park Road, Dingle.
■ Electronic waves which stimulate the muscles in the skin, stretching and toning the face.
■ Margi, brave enough to be pictured without a scrap of make-up, said: "Well, when a girl hits 40, you have to start taking evasive action and I'd love to get rid of my wrinkles."
■ She added: "Sandra is brilliant. She's won loads of awards, and is my emergency hairdresser. Now she's giving me a new face ready for my new Good Sex Guide."
■ Margi is all set for a course of ten treatments at the salon, so keep watching the *ECHO* for her transformation.
■ Meanwhile, she has given herself another birthday lift with a Wonderbody — the all-in-one version of the Wonderbra.

● *Women's TV trials — page 12*

● Very uplifting . . . Margi models the Wonderbody

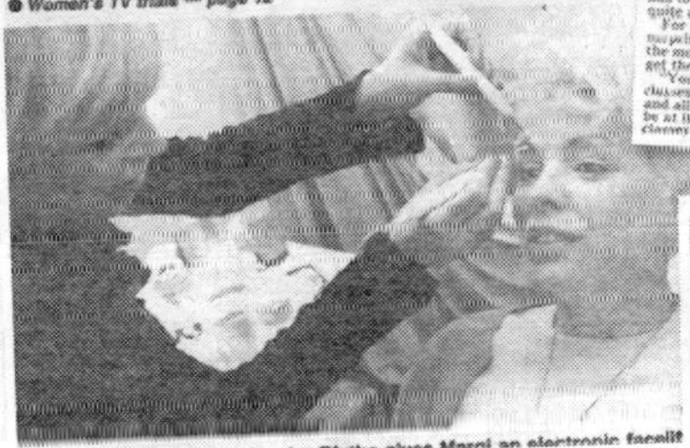

● Birthday treat . . . Sandra Blythe gives Margi an electronic facelift

The SEX QUEENIE!

Margi's back and guess what's high on her New Year agenda

☐ *Everything you wanted to know about sex . . . Margi Clarke on our screens soon with The Good Sex Guide — and with a new series of Making Out*

by HANNAH STEPHENSON

THE BRIGHT red lipstick and peroxide hair are as unmistakable as the thick Scouse accent and brazen banter.

Margi Clarke, the actress who ... in the hit film *Letter To Brezhnev*, and then as the irrepressible Queenie in TV's *Making Out*, is back — and she's concentrating on a subject close to her heart . . . sex.

For she's host of ITV's **The Good Sex Guide** — starting on Monday January 11 — which mixes factual information and expert advice, with real people's revelations and a host of comedy sketches.

Nitty-gritty

"It's ground-breaking," she enthuses. "I'm leading a verbal sexual revolution. There's a Berlin wall around sex and Margi Clarke's gonna knock it down.

"I've always played characters who are interested in sex. I'm interested in sex and it's such a gift to us all — you don't have to be of any class system to enjoy sex. You don't have to be attractive."

In fact Margi had no trouble getting people to offload their sexual experiences and problems on her — they were positively queuing up to get down to the nitty-gritty of their sex lives on screen.

And although you may think that there's not much you could teach this incorrigible, warm-hearted woman about sex, she has to confess that she did learn quite a bit.

For a starter, she was surprised at finding out that it's the most unlikely people who get the most pleasure out of sex.

"You think because the upper classes have all that freedom and all that money, that they'll be at it, you think the working classes will be at it because they ...

"I went to a middle-class house in suburbia in Manchester and it shocked me because it was stuffed to the gills with sex toys!"

Professional advice is given in the seven-part series by consultants, psychologists and sex counsellors, but there are also sketches performed by some of Britain's top comedy actors and household names.

Upper-crust actress Helena Bonham-Carter was just one of the stars to open Margi's eyes.

"I didn't know she was going to appear on the programme. You need a bit of the upper class taking part. Sex is an ...

... and provocative appearance, you could be forgiven for mistaking Margi for a wayward woman — but far from it.

She has a 17-year-old son Laurence, the product of a teenage marriage which didn't last, and an eight-month-old daughter Rowan through her 13-year partnership with artist Jamie Reid, designer of the Sex Pistols' graphics. They live happily in Wavertree.

Comfortable

But doing **The Good Sex Guide** sparked a lot of interest from her other half.

"When I'd go home at night ...

She is as comfortable talking about sex as she would be talking about the weather — yet says she never had any sexual conversation with her parents when she was younger.

Her father was a Liverpool docker and her mother a Labour councillor, and as one of 10 children, Margi learned she had to shout loud to make her presence felt.

She says her mother fully approves of her doing the programme, but will probably get some stick from the neighbours about her daughter presenting it.

But it was something most ...

— what about if me mother sees it? Everybody's mother's got to be out on the same night — when this programme goes out."

She feels for teenagers growing up in today's society.

"I feel sorry for the kids. That was the one thing. I wasn't shocked by anything — I'm 37 years of age, and you're not going to be shocked by much — but I was really surprised that young people are so naive. They can't experiment.

"They are having sex with fear. You and I didn't. I mean our only fear was getting pregnant. That wasn't so bad — but fear of death is."

Margi's message to those mums and dads who are sceptical about letting their teenagers watch this programme is clear.

"If parents have got any sense, they are far better to let their children watch it. It's not embarrassing. It's not salacious."

She feels the show should perhaps have incorporated the views of old people — and may do if there's a second series.

"If you speak to people who've had their sex life, they're the ones who can tell young people how they achieved it and how they managed to stay in relationships for a long, long time."

And what does her 17-year-old son think of mom talking openly about sex? "He understands. He's more upset about me swearing. Far more upset than my parents ever were."

Madonna

Margi is quick to praise other women who have brought sex out into the open, such as Madonna: "She's brought the subject on to the coffee tables of the world."

Sex is high on Margi's agenda in 1993. In February she will be embarking on "a one-woman sex show" which she will be taking ...

Christmas in Kirkby – now that's magic!

... on her way to the Empire Theatre.

Margi to star in the Empire panto

by Penny Kiley

For Margi is to play the Fairy Godmother in the Liverpool Empire production of Cinderella.

Cinderella opens at the Empire Theatre on December 12.

Making Out for two

☐ Margi as Queenie: "She's a great character — brash, tough, outrageous, with a heart of gold."

Kirkby girl Margi is a mum-to-be on and off screen

By Huw Rossiter

SHE'S been described as the Marilyn Monroe of Merseyside, but there's nothing "actressy" about Margi Clarke.

Extrovert

Great fan

Thank Yous

All my family, the Barretts and to my children, Laurence and Rowan and the Clarkes: Our Marion, Eileen, Frank, Jane, Muriel and Angela

Jamie Reid

My aunties Kathleen Phillips and Muriel
Uncle Patsy, Uncle Teddy, Maria Haver, my nephews and nieces
The O'Dowd Family
Gregory Husband, Francis Husband and John Husband (that's a lot of husbands)
Adam Clarke
Jane Bester and Lewis Bester
Harvey Clarke
Cheryl Cooper and family
Grandma Nora, Grandad Jack Reid and Uncle Bruce Reid
Laura (Rowen's sister)
The man who brought me into television ,the late, great Tony Wilson

My agents old and new:
Lou Coulson
Elizabeth Stocking
Anne Moore

ACKNOWLEDGEMENTS

Clapperboard director Maureen Sinclair – for keeping dreams alive for young dreamers

Cathy Roberts, the captain of the tug on the Mersey The France Hayhurst where this book was written.
Yes, it was REALLY written on the river Mersey

My literary helpmate Peter Grant

Willy and Annie Russell
Carol Ann Duffy – Our Poet Laureate
The sadly (every day missed) Adrian Henri

The Trinity Mirror Press Gang

Bad Cop, Dynamic Steve, Cuddly Ken, Cookie Babe and publishing Guru Dicko – from the Manchester days. They are the 'A' Team along with: Zoe (Faye), Vicky the Stitcher and Colin Harrison. James Cleary for saying: "What does this mean...are you sure she wants this in?" Michael 'The Sharp Suit' McGuinness and who can forget Kags Cadman; Liz Morgan and Claire 'Keyring' Brown. And Och, Amelia

Photographer: Stephen Shakeshaft

Anthony Barrett, Maria Barrett
Marion Macgregor Reid

Alan Gill
Derek Dunbar
Jon Savage
Geoff Moore,
TV supremo David Liddiment

Daily Post and ECHO picture men – past and present.
That ace Andrew Teebay's a fab snapper, and many thanks to Head of
Images, Barrie Mills.

And there's more...

My dearly departed bessie mate Kathleen Johno

Carleen Lundon
The Beatles
Henry Epstein
The late, great Ken Campbell
Mark McNulty
Gerry Butler
Our Mo's Dominic
Brain (Chunky) Hibberd from Making Out
Tim Healy
Kelly Brook

Arthur Dooley
Pete Sheldon
Charlie Castleton
Shaun McKenna
Gerry Potter
Glennis Davies
Paul Gascoigne
Liz Dawn
Mike McCartney
Allan Williams (he was instrumental with The Beatles and me)
Jake and Marie Abrahams
Tony Hennigan
The Zinc

ACKNOWLEDGEMENTS

Jimmy Flynn
Nicky Johnson picture man

Tony Benn
Joe Strummer
Rhys Mwyn
Dave Hughes

The legendary friend Brian King
Stephen Pietri and Muriel Cleek
Sandi Hughes
Leah McCormack
Angela Pepper
Arthur Scargill
Martin O'Shea
KLF and Bill Drummond
Michael Nicols
Phillip Dresner
Patrick Jacquin

MY dear departed Uncle Barney

John and Cunard Yank Uncle Frank

The staff of Lewis'
Damien Hirst
Gabby Hurst
The Glitter nan Judy Blane
George Michael
Malcolm McLaren
Vivienne Westwood

Rowan's surrogate grandma
Pattie Dawson
Lucy Dawson
Joey Donaghue
Jenny O'Shea
All my school friends from Sacred Heart and St Gregory's
Littlewoods Pools
Love to our Welsh family the Davies' on the Great Orme
David Icke
Dennis Murphy
Steve Jones
Martin of Herberts
Keith's in Lark Lane
Christine Tremarco
Nurse Katie Sheldon and family

Sorry if I've got your name wrong. I know who you are and you know who you are.
   To all the people not mentioned in this book – thanks...
   I'll see you in the sequel!
   Ta for everybody who has helped me get to where I am.
   And much love to ALL absent friends.

Margi Mary Bernadette Clarke 2010

Index

NOW YOU DON'T

Now that you've seen me

In plain sight, full view

It's how to become

VISIBLE

And break through

ANEW…

A poem by
Margaret Mary Bernadette Clarke

Also available from Trinity Mirror Media

£14.99

£9.99

Tune into Billy's life story –
the lad-next-door and multi-
award winning broadcaster

A magical history tour back to
Lennon's roots – with new
research and rare archive photos

£6.75

£9.99

The real Sir Paul McCartney and
the secrets of his childhood and
early life in Liverpool

Author Ken Rogers brings
the golden memories of his
childhood alive

To buy any of these titles, or for a great range of other books,
photographs and more, visit MERSEYSHOP.com or call 0845 143 0001

Also available from Trinity Mirror Media

£6.99

£14.99

The ultimate Liverpool guide book, written by the award-winning journalists of the Daily Post & Echo

Featuring over 100 recipes – a real flavour of the world in one city. A must for anyone who loves food and loves Liverpool

£6.75

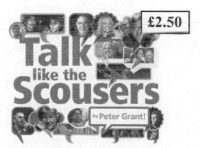

£2.50

This brilliant autobiography will make you laugh, make you cry & inspire you

This pocket book is a celebration of the accent and the phrases

To buy any of these titles, or for a great range of other books, photographs and more, visit MERSEYSHOP.com or call 0845 143 0001

This book is dedicated to my brother
Michael, sister Kathleen
and baby Joan